*"The inheritance I would leave
to my nation is that they
conduct themselves so as to merit
the smile of the Great Spirit,
which watches over the red man
and the pale face."*

— KIOWA CHIEF YELLOW WOLF, 1863

Trail to

Wounded Knee

THE LAST STAND OF THE PLAINS INDIANS
1860-1890

HERMAN J. VIOLA

NATIONAL GEOGRAPHIC
WASHINGTON, D.C.

Contents

✳

Through six years in the West, artist George Catlin captured authentic Indian scenes like this "Buffalo Chase Over Prairie Bluffs," painted in 1832-33.

PAGE 1: *A pre-1790 Indian pictograph depicts a warrior carrying a battle shield.*

PAGES 2-3: *Feather, thread, and cloth express a prayer on a medicine tree in southwest Montana.*

Four generations of a Sioux family in 1906 show the Plains Indians' transformation.
Chief Two Strike holds his great-granddaughter and sits beside his son, Little Hawk.
His grandson, Poor Boy, stands behind him, well on his way along the white man's road.

Foreword

✳

The one major lesson I've learned in my long life is that it is not easy being an Indian. Once this realization is forced upon you by negative elements, both real and imagined, its strength grows within you and increasingly takes over your life. This perception is exasperating though ultimately rewarding, because it does save you many years of searching for yourself by providing a goal, a dedicated direction to do what you can to right this ancient wrong. As my life's plan switched from the defensive to the offensive, I encountered remarkable success in the areas I can influence, thanks to the Indian world I deeply believe in, and the friends I met along the way. One of the more remarkable of these people is the author of this book. Like most interesting things, our relationship has a history that began long ago when our hair still retained some color and we took long strides. On occasion, we now sit around talking about those long-ago days and chuckle at our youthful enthusiasm.

While I was attending the University of California at Berkeley in 1970, another phase of my lifelong goal emerged. Having access to the numerous academic resources there, I began to locate and collect all that had been written on my tribe—the A'aninin Gros Ventre Indian people—because we had no such materials on our Indian reservation in Montana. The ongoing search eventually carried me to Washington, D.C., four years later, where I met Dr. Herman Viola for the first time. His lifetime interest in the American Indian people allowed him, as the director of the National Anthropological Archives, to establish a tribal historian project within the hallowed halls of the elite Smithsonian Institution, and I signed up as one of its first entrants.

The intervening years have been kind to us as we each continued our respective journeys. My search for cultural justice took a quantum leap in 1989, when Congress passed the National Museum of the American Indian Act, and soon after work began on building the museum that will tell the world the true stories of the American Indian and what happened to us. I soon signed up and we moved to the East Coast in 1994, to help with this lifetime goal and enjoy a rare period when a dream actually becomes a reality.

Herman and I visit more often now, and I am impressed how busy and productive he continues to be. Over the years his interest evolved into a firm dedication, and he has visited most of Indian country and has Indian people as friends everywhere. His relationships with us are not limited to an occasional handshake or colorful greeting card at Christmas; they go much deeper—like family. He knows the names of our family members and other relatives, knows the progress of our health—and we know of his as well. So, amidst all of this, I am once again impressed by his authorship on a subject that we both love: the American Indian people.

With his long familiarity in the western Indian people and their lives, in this book Dr. Viola has focused on a tough 30-year period and divided it into geographical and dramatic sections. Each of the book's eight chapters addresses notable events in the Indian history of the West, introduced by a statement from an Indian participant of the time. The author has taken the main stories, enhanced them with first-person accounts from both the Indian and the non-Indian, and woven them together into a complex fabric.

The stories revolve around the persistent efforts to own the Indian people's land and to get rid of us. After fleeing European injustice and landing on the East Coast of this country, white settlers—Christian, churchgoing people—began to remove the Indian people and take over the land they had occupied for centuries. Removal could take place by any means possible: either by forced banishment or by a musket ball. The killings usually included not only men, but the women and children as well. This same blind, driving greed became the official law of the land as federal policy, when under Andrew Jackson's administration Congress passed the Indian Removal Act of 1830.

The federal government soon removed some of the Five Civilized Tribes westward. Seven years later, although the Cherokee people had won the right to their land in a Supreme Court decision, Jackson used armed troops to force the tribe westward to Oklahoma on the infamous Trail of Tears. Nearly 4,000 Indian people, including women and children, died on the 800-mile enforced march.

This official, sustained, unjust policy was implemented in many places. It affected tribes across the country, poisoning their relationship not only to the United States government but to the beneficiaries of the program as well: the non-Indians. As the Indian patriots struggled to protect their lands and their very lives from the invaders, their conflicts with the Americans soon turned to armed combat. No other honorable avenue was open to them. Justice was on an extended vacation, because no matter how just or noble their cause, the Indians always ultimately lost.

*I*n this book, we follow their doomed struggle, beginning with the hopeful Southern Plains delegation to Washington, D.C., in 1863, made by leaders of the Kiowa, Comanche, Cheyenne, Arapaho, and Caddo tribes. The author takes us along with them and paints a vivid picture of all the active and noisy interactions in the nation's capital. It often feels like we are in the same room with them.

Upon returning home, the Cheyenne and Arapaho find their people still hungry and desperately seeking food by any possible means, including raiding. The settlers in Colorado inform Washington, D.C., of their concerns, and soon Colonel Chivington, a former Methodist clergyman, is designated to head 700 volunteers. On November 28, 1864, they attack a peaceful Cheyenne camp that is under the protection of not only an American flag but a white flag of truce. They continue their rampage and slaughter and mutilate hundreds of Indian people, again mostly women and children. These killings are known as the Sand Creek Massacre of 1864.

FOLLOWING PAGES:
Inspired by George Catlin, Philadelphia artist Charles Deas traveled west, then settled in St. Louis, painting scenes of American Indian life including this 1845 oil painting, "A Group of Sioux."

The author also introduces us to the great Sioux leaders Red Cloud and Crazy Horse. We rejoice in their victories along the Bozeman Trail, in spite of the Westerners' hatred of them. The Westerners could vote, but the Indian people, who had lived in this land for thousands of years, did not yet enjoy that privilege. With no political voice, they were ignored. They would have to wait nearly 60 more years to vote as Americans. So the politicians, and therefore the government, continued to turn a deaf ear to their complaints. They usually ignored the treaties they had signed with the Indians when it suited them to do so. And the pragmatic injustices prevailed.

As I found myself traveling along with the Southern Plains Indian warriors on their way to prison at Fort Marion, Florida, after fighting for their homeland, I felt both sorrow and pride. Leaving one's family is always painful, but I knew that they would survive and go on to develop traditional artistic skills at Fort Marion and Hampton. Some, I knew, would ultimately learn new skills at the Carlisle Indian School in Pennsylvania where, one day in 1912, would emerge a Sauk and Fox Indian man named Jim Thorpe, often called the world's greatest athlete. These wonderfully written stories of a tragic time in our history often gather me up and carry me away, even though these are not new paths for me. After reading about the horrors of Sand Creek and what happened to the proud Chief Joseph and the Nez Perce people, I have to stop, take a deep breath, and wipe the tears from my eyes until the internal rage within me subsides. But then my heart soars as I ride a spotted pony across the prairie at full speed next to Crazy Horse as he blows his eagle wing bone whistle, taunting the soldiers of the Seventh Cavalry. Dr. Viola has the distinct advantage of viewing these events more historically and objectively than I do, since as an Indian person I am part of the story and enjoy no such bounds.

This round of Indian stories ends on a religious note, as it should. As their world continued to come crashing down on them, the Indian people became increasingly desperate, seeking relief from any quarter. In the late 1880s, word came across the prairie grass that a Paiute holy man had a vision and went to heaven. He learned that if the Indian people prayed, were nice to each other, and

performed certain dances to special songs, three things would happen: Their deceased ancestors would return, the vanished buffalo would once again fill the countryside, and the white people would go away. Upon his return to this world, Wovoka, as the holy man was called, spread the eagerly welcomed word, and the messianic message moved from tribe to tribe.

After the Sioux people received the word, many of them joined the Ghost Dance, as the movement was called. Government officials became worried and fearful of the militant warriors within that tribe and tried to control them. As he was being arrested, Chief Sitting Bull was assassinated. The Army restrained Chief Big Foot, who was sick, and his followers, who were under a white flag. When a shot rang out, the troops opened fire with cannons and other weapons. The warriors returned the fire as best they could. When the blizzard cleared after that frigid winter day, December 29, 1890, near Wounded Knee, South Dakota, the frozen bodies of the fallen were revealed. Tribal members say the U.S. Army killed over 400 of their people, not sparing women and children, of course. For their deeds on the killing fields of Wounded Knee, 18 soldiers were awarded congressional Medals of Honor.

Whenever I read or remember this tragic and painful segment of our history, I am filled with anger and sadness that tempers and hardens my resolve with dedication. It is a trip we all should take. Through this pain, though, is also pride and honor, which make us like no other people on this earth. We are very special, but it is not easy, because we are still under pressure from various sources.

Some good things have been happening to us for a change. When the National Museum of the American Indian opens its doors on the National Mall in September 2004, we can at long last tell our true story to the world. The new museum is already doing many good things, one of the latest being to sponsor an inaugural powwow on the Mall in September 2002, where Dr. Herman Viola, among others, was honored for his work in the Indian world.

We can never forget what happened to us and why. We must tell our children, for this knowledge will strengthen and carry them through to the future as a people. The Jewish people suffered much pain and loss in the Holocaust, and they will never forget, for it keeps them together, too. Americans will never forget Pearl Harbor or September 11 for the same reason. Strengthened by the sad memories of Sand Creek, Wounded Knee, and all the others, we owe it to our ancestors, our children, and those to come to continue our proud march as Indian people to our honorable destiny. Herman, thanks for telling it like it really was and always will be. ↩

Chief Joseph, the heroic Nez Perce leader, counseled peace but was forced into war. He led the Nez Perce through vigilant efforts to escape the U.S. Army in 1877. In those days called the "Red Napoleon" by the media, in later years he became a sad-eyed old man.

— GEORGE P. HORSE CAPTURE
Senior Counselor to the Director
NATIONAL MUSEUM OF THE AMERICAN INDIAN

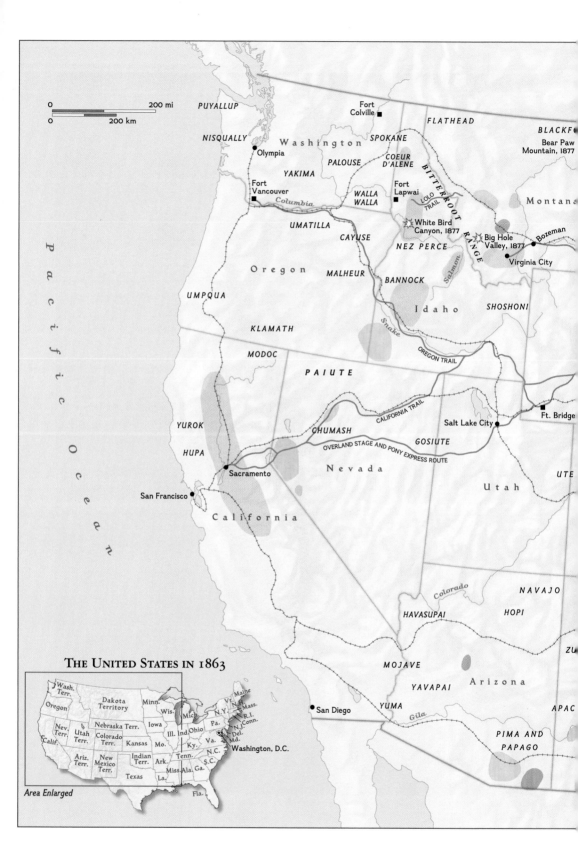

PUYALLUP

NISQUALLY

Washington

Olympia

Fort
Vancouver

Columbia

YAKIMA

Fort
Colville

SPOKANE

PALOUSE

COEUR
D'ALENE

WALLA
WALLA

FLATHEAD

BLACKF

Bear Paw
Mountain, 1877

M o n t a n a

Fort
Lapwai

LOLO
TRAIL

BITTERROOT RANGE

UMATILLA

O r e g o n

MALHEUR

CAYUSE

NEZ PERCE

White Bird
Canyon, 1877

Salmon

Big Hole
Valley, 1877

Virginia City

Bozeman

UMPQUA

BANNOCK

I d a h o

SHOSHONI

KLAMATH

Snake

MODOC

PAIUTE

OREGON TRAIL

YUROK

HUPA

Sacramento

CHUMASH

CALIFORNIA TRAIL

OVERLAND STAGE AND PONY EXPRESS ROUTE

GOSIUTE

Salt Lake City

Ft. Bridge

UTE

N e v a d a

U t a h

San Francisco

C a l i f o r n i a

P a c i f i c   O c e a n

Colorado

NAVAJO

HAVASUPAI

HOPI

ZU

MOJAVE

A r i z o n a

YAVAPAI

YUMA

San Diego

Gila

APAC

PIMA AND
PAPAGO

0   200 mi
0   200 km

The United States in 1863

Wash.
Terr.

Oregon

Dakota
Territory

Minn.

Wis.

Mich.

Vt. Maine
N.H.
N.Y. Mass.
R.I.
Pa.
N.J. Conn.
Del.
Md.

Nev.
Terr.

Utah
Terr.

Nebraska Terr.

Iowa

Ill. Ind. Ohio

Ky.

Va.

Calif.

Colorado
Terr.

Kansas

Mo.

Washington, D.C.

Ariz.
Terr.

New
Mexico
Terr.

Indian
Terr.

Ark.

Tenn.

N.C.

Miss. Ala. Ga.

S.C.

Texas

La.

Fla.

Area Enlarged

14

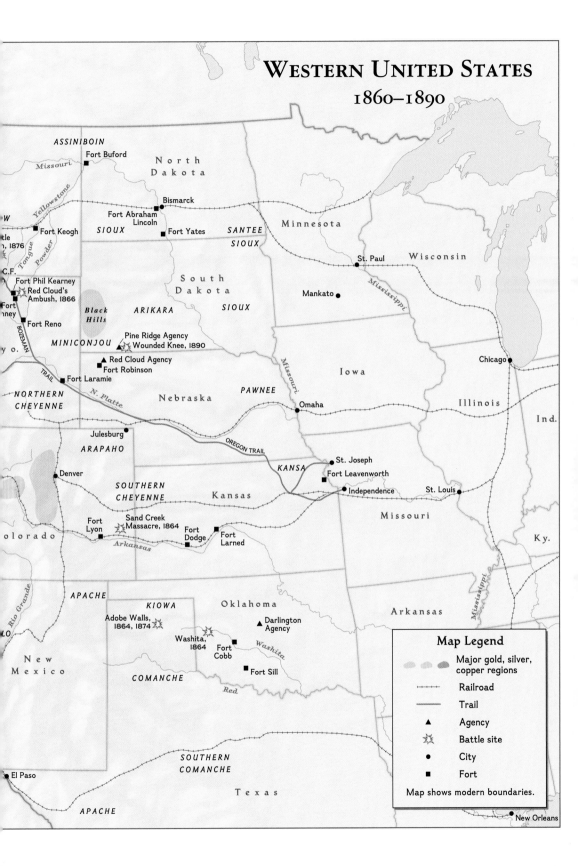

WESTERN UNITED STATES
1860–1890

ASSINIBOIN

Fort Buford ■

North
Dakota

Missouri

Bismarck ●

Fort Abraham
Lincoln

W

tle
n, 1876

■ Fort Keogh

C.F.

Yellowstone

Tongue

Powder

SIOUX

Fort Yates ■

SANTEE
SIOUX

Minnesota

St. Paul ●

Wisconsin

Mississippi

Fort Phil Kearney
Red Cloud's
Ambush, 1866

Fort
ney

■ Fort Reno

BOZEMAN

y o.

TRAIL

South
Dakota

Black
Hills

ARIKARA

SIOUX

Mankato ●

MINICONJOU

▲ Pine Ridge Agency
Wounded Knee, 1890

Chicago ●

▲ Red Cloud Agency
Fort Robinson

Iowa

Illinois

NORTHERN
CHEYENNE

■ Fort Laramie

N. Platte

Nebraska

PAWNEE

Omaha ●

Ind.

Julesburg ●

ARAPAHO

OREGON TRAIL

Missouri

Denver ●

SOUTHERN
CHEYENNE

KANSA

St. Joseph ●
Fort Leavenworth ■

St. Louis ●

Kansas

Independence ●

Missouri

Ky.

Fort
Lyon ■

Sand Creek
Massacre, 1864

Fort
Dodge ■

Fort
Larned ■

Arkansas

olorado

APACHE

KIOWA

Oklahoma

Arkansas

Mississippi

Rio Grande

LO

Adobe Walls,
1864, 1874

Darlington
Agency ▲

New
Mexico

Washita,
1864

Fort
Cobb

Washita

■ Fort Sill

COMANCHE

Red

El Paso ●

SOUTHERN
COMANCHE

APACHE

Texas

New Orleans ●

Map Legend

Major gold, silver,
copper regions

Railroad

Trail

▲ Agency

✳ Battle site

● City

■ Fort

Map shows modern boundaries.

"Tell them that I have seen their 'Great Father,' and that he has promised to take care of the red man."

— Yellow Wolf, on his deathbed in Washington, D.C.

the Southern Plains Indian Delegation

Into the 1860s, Plains Indians lived in tepee villages that could move with the game and the seasons, like this Cheyenne camp in Kansas Territory—so different from the reservation lifestyle into which they would be forced in decades to come.

1863

✳

On March 21, 1863, a steam locomotive chugged into the Washington, D.C., railway station, pulling a car full of unforgettable passengers. On board, a delegation of 16 Indians—14 men and 2 women—had traveled from their homelands in the Colorado Territory. Their trip to the nation's capital had taken more than a month. They traveled first by horseback, then by wagon, with a U.S. Cavalry escort for protection, then boarded the Washington-bound train at Fort Larned, Kansas. Their rail adventure followed a tedious, circuitous route, dictated by the realities of the ongoing Civil War: from Kansas through St. Louis, Chicago, Buffalo, New York, and Baltimore. It was indeed a time of national crisis, but the Civil War in fact inspired the very invitation for them to come. Understandably nervous about their first train ride, the members of the 1863 delegation quickly came to enjoy the "iron horse" and were excited to finally reach Washington—called in Plains Indian sign language "the home of our father where we go on the puffing wagon to council."

These members of the 1863 delegation to Washington were the Who's Who of four proud and powerful Indian tribes of the Southern Plains—the Kiowa, Comanche, Cheyenne, and Arapaho—with a Caddo representative included for good measure. The most prominent delegates were Ten Bears of the Comanche, Lone Wolf and White Bear (better known as Satanta) of the Kiowa, and Lean Bear of the Cheyenne. The two women were Coy, the wife of White Bear, and Etla, the wife of Lone Wolf. Yellow Wolf of the Kiowa, the eldest member of the delegation, attracted the most attention because of the large silver Thomas Jefferson peace medal he wore around his neck. Accompanying this distinguished group were several white people, including federal Indian agent Samuel G. Colley, his wife, and their son, paid to be an assistant on the journey.

Although the Indian women had no official duties while in Washington, their presence was all part of the standard delegation script. The ladies of the capital would escort their female visitors to sites such as schools and churches, hoping that they would return to their people

PRECEDING PAGES: *Buffalo could stop a train, but they could not stop progress, as suggested in N. H. Trotter's 1897 painting, "Held Up."*

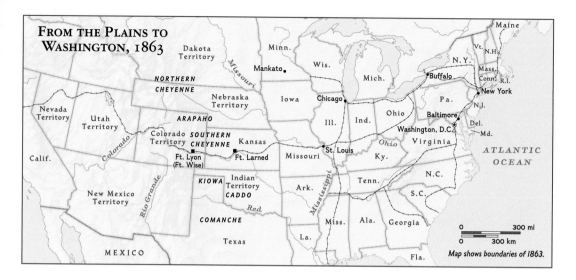

FROM THE PLAINS TO WASHINGTON, 1863

Map shows boundaries of 1863.

As Cheyenne members of the 1863 delegation prepared to leave Kansas for Washington, opposite, they were photographed with their Indian agent in Fort Leavenworth; left to right: agent Samuel G. Colley, War Bonnet, Standing in the Water, and Lean Bear.

impressed with the white woman's ways. Indeed a primary purpose behind most of the Indian delegations invited to Washington was to impress Native American leaders with the wonders of white civilization: To educate them by sharing culture and knowledge and to convince them that capitulation and assimilation might be the best way for them to respond as the white world moved in on their lands.

All along the way during their railroad trip, crowds, sometimes hostile, had lined up at train stations to see the car full of Indians passing through. The Indians were unaccustomed to a world full of white people— it seemed impossible that there could be so many! According to an agent with a later delegation, the Indians in his care solved among themselves the mystery of how so many white people could appear outside the car in town after town. Just as their people relocated their villages from site to site, the Indians reasoned, so these must be the same white people every time, using their superior technology to move their city with them.

The highlight of the 1863 delegation's visit was the meeting with President Abraham Lincoln at the White House on March 27. A large crowd awaited them there—the secretaries of State, Treasury, the Navy, and the Interior, the ministers of England, France, Prussia, and Brazil, and their families jammed the East Room. The nervous Indian delegates sat at one end of the long room, facing the restless spectators. Despite the best efforts of Lincoln's secretary, John Nicolay, there was a considerable amount of pushing and shoving to get a close look at the Indians.

"There unfortunately seems to be an incurable habit among the good people of our country in the house of the Chief Magistrate to press forward and not give an inch to those behind," lamented one reporter.

"Everybody seemed to find someone's bonnet or shoulder in the way, and to think himself or herself entitled to the best and most conspicuous place. . . . Still everything went off very well," wrote another. "These Indians are fine-looking men. They have all the hard and cruel lines in their faces which we might expect in savages; but they are evidently men of intelligence and force of character. They were both dignified and cordial in their manner, and listened to everything with great interest."

President Lincoln entered the room. Each of the chiefs gave him a quick, vigorous handshake. The President turned to their interpreter, John S. Smith, and said, "Say to them I am very glad to see them, and if they have anything to say, it will afford me great pleasure to hear them."

It was remarkable that Lincoln took the time to greet an Indian delegation at this moment in history. The war gave him little time for such diplomatic chores. It was March 1863, two years into the Civil War, and the Union did not yet have the upper hand. The Emancipation Proclamation had gone into effect at the beginning of the year, but not

FOLLOWING PAGES: Shimmering gold stands of tall grass such as this stretched for miles across the Plains, a swath of the North American midlands stretching from Canada to Texas.

During the 1862 Indian uprising in Minnesota, Little Crow and his Santee followers, angry over the government's failure to provide food as promised, killed hundreds of settlers. Frightened white refugees fled the wrath of vengeful warriors.

until summer would the tide turn in military favor toward the North, after Lee ordered a retreat from the Battle of Gettysburg and Grant took Vicksburg on the Mississippi River.

Another war was looming on the American horizon in the 1860s, though: the war between white settlers and American Indians, fought over Western lands and resources. In fact, the struggle between North and South over issues of economics and slavery had a tremendous impact on the life and future of American Indians. Tribes east of the Mississippi were drawn into the conflict because both the North and South sought Indian recruits for their armies. Confederate agents sought alliances with tribes in the Far West, hoping that Indians might supply them with much-needed horses, help secure a supply route, and cause enough trouble to divert some of the North's military forces from the eastern theater. Not much encouragement was needed, because many of the western tribes, particularly the buffalo-hunting peoples on the Great Plains, were already angry about the hordes of white trespassers on their hunting grounds.

Gold and silver rushes made the Colorado Territory a hot spot

In the 1840s, white settlers started moving west through the Plains (opposite), regardless of the people already living in those lands.

waiting to explode. By the outbreak of the Civil War, as many as 100,000 whites had already elbowed their way into Colorado, dislocating and angering the Cheyenne, Arapaho, Kiowa, Comanche, Ute, and other resident tribes. Ever since the Oregon Trail opened and gold was discovered in California, the U.S. government had been trying to clear Indians out of the paths of settlers and prospectors moving west. The government designated lands to the north and south of the great westward corridor as Indian reserves, promising some support to tribes who moved within those boundaries. Through the Treaty of Fort Wise, signed in February 1861, the federal government offered the Cheyenne and Arapaho a small reservation in southeastern Colorado. But scattered bands of warriors ignored the treaty and began harassing wagon trains, mining camps, and stagecoach lines. Confederate officers added fuel to the fire by attempting to befriend the Kiowa and Comanche, guardians of the Southern Plains.

In Minnesota, the Santee Sioux had peaceably moved onto reservation lands, expecting to receive the supplies promised by officials. Preoccupied with the war, though, the federal government fell short on its commitments. Hungry Santees came to a local trading post, seeking food, and someone heard a trader shout out, "Let them eat grass." Frustrated and bitter over broken promises, the Santee rose up to reclaim their land. U.S. troops, led by Gen. John Pope, just defeated at the Battle of Bull Run, arrived in Minnesota to find some 500 settlers already killed. Panic was so widespread that some 23 counties in southwest Minnesota were all but depopulated. Officials arrested 2,000 Indians, sentenced 303 to death, and and ultimately executed 38 of them. Fear and animosity spread through white communities across the West.

Indian concerns were administered by the Bureau of Indian Affairs, part of the Department of the Interior, through a network of superintendencies and agencies. Federal Indian agents had direct management of one or more tribes on a reservation. Agent Colley, who accompanied the 1863 delegation east, was stationed in the Colorado Territory at Fort Lyon. Sensing that Confederates were making gains among the Southern Plains Indians, Colley had urged his superiors to invite leaders of the more militant tribes to Washington.

"I am fearful that unless something is done soon for these tribes," he wrote in September 1862, "they will cause us much trouble and probably cut off communication between the States and New Mexico." John Evans, governor of the Colorado Territory, forwarded the request to William P. Dole, Commissioner of Indian Affairs, who happened to be Colley's cousin. Dole quickly approved it.

In punishment for their uprising, 38 Santee Sioux were executed at Mankato, Minnesota, on December 26, 1862, as depicted in this lithograph by John C. Wise. Of the 2,000 arrested, Lincoln commuted many sentences, but at least one who died had warned white friends to seek safety.

Washington delegations had long been a mainstay of government Indian policy. Diplomacy, intimidation, even bribery were preferred over military force when dealing with truculent tribes, and often the tactics worked. After meeting the Great Father, being showered with presents and attention, then inspecting military installations, most tribal leaders went home with profound respect for American power. "A forest of guns," marveled more than one chief after seeing the Washington arsenal. Almost everything on the agenda was calculated to impress, intimidate, or persuade. The ultimate goal was to convince the delegates to take up the white man's road: to give up their way of life for agriculture or some other occupation more acceptable to the white community.

Delegation chiefs received many gifts, the most important being peace medals, a tradition dating back to French and Spanish explorers. From George Washington to Benjamin Harrison, every President except John Adams presented Indian delegates with silver medallions that carried the full weight of national allegiance. The largest medals, about three inches in diameter, went to the head chief; the smaller ones went to chiefs and warriors of lesser rank.

The face of each medal bore the current President's silhouette—in this case, Lincoln's. The reverse for all the medals from Jefferson to Zachary Taylor carried hands clasped in friendship, a symbol that appeared on many other gifts for the Indians, such as silver-plated tomahawks and pipes. The Lincoln reverse, though, carried a more ominous image. An Indian in a war bonnet plows his fields while another Indian scalps a fallen enemy: The pair of images was supposed to show the advantages of civilized life, but the medal succeeding only in arousing the animosity of humanitarians of the day.

Out West, the very idea of Indian delegations raised more than a few hackles. "Instead of taking delegations of savages to Washington, at enormous expense," fumed the editor of the *Weekly Rocky Mountain News*, "would it not be better to . . . wipe the treacherous vagabonds from the face of the earth? The experiences of the past year, in Minnesota and elsewhere, afford the most positive evidence of the brutal and treacherous character of the Indian tribes. They seem to feel no gratitude for the liberal manner in which the Government has provided them with the necessaries and comforts of life, and do not hesitate to violate the most solemn treaties."

Despite such attitudes in the West, those in Washington did their best to greet the Indian delegates warmly. In response to President Lincoln's greeting, Lean Bear, a chief representing the Cheyenne, spoke first for the delegation. The powerful and vigorous warrior was so nervous that he asked to sit while addressing the Great Father, which amused the audience. All fell silent, though, when Lean Bear began to speak. He proved to be a fluent and animated orator.

"The President is the Great Chief of the White People," Lean Bear declared. "I am the Great Chief of the Indians. Our wigwams are not so fine as this; they are small and poor. I hope the Great Chief will look upon his people with favor, and say in his wisdom what would be best for them to do. We are here to listen to his advice and carry it in our hearts . . . I will hear all the Great Chief has to say; and when I go away I will not carry [his words] in my pocket, but in my heart, where they will not be lost." Lean Bear then informed President Lincoln of the many white people moving into his country. The Indians wished to live in peace, he continued, but he feared the white people did not share that wish.

After meeting President Lincoln, members of the 1863 delegation posed in the White House conservatory. In the front row, left to right, sit War Bonnet, Standing in the Water, Lean Bear, and Yellow Wolf. Within 18 months all four were dead, Yellow Wolf in Washington and the others in attacks on their villages.

THE SOUTHERN PLAINS INDIAN DELEGATION

Regardless, he would keep his warriors from the war path—unless the white men provoked a fight.

Spotted Wolf, another Cheyenne, rose to tell President Lincoln that he was surprised at the friendliness of the white people. Everywhere he went, said Spotted Wolf, he found only brothers. He said that he was also amazed at all the wonderful things the delegates had seen during their visit to the U.S. capital. "When I look about me and see all these fine things, it seems like some kind of magic. I do not even know how I got here, so far away from home. It seems to me that I must have come on wings like a bird through the air."

Then Lincoln addressed the delegation. "You have all spoken of the strange sights you see here, among your pale-faced brethren," he said. "But you have seen but a very small part of the pale-faced people. There are people in this wigwam, now looking at you, who have come from other countries a great deal farther off than you have come." He launched into a geography lesson and, as he spoke, an attendant placed a large globe of the world in front of the delegates. Lincoln informed the Indians that

the world was a great ball and that visitors in the East Room had come from all parts of that ball.

Lincoln then introduced Joseph Henry, the first secretary of the Smithsonian Institution. Henry gave a detailed explanation of the formation of the earth, as understood in 1863. He used the globe to point out the oceans, the various countries represented by visitors in the room, and the location of Washington in relation to the homeland of the Indians on the American continent.

When Henry finished speaking, Lincoln resumed his remarks. He told the Indians they would have to change their way of life if they wished to become as prosperous as the white man. Whites, he explained, cultivated the soil and relied on bread rather than game for subsistence. Whites were a peaceful people: "We are not, as a race, so much disposed to fight and kill one another as our red brethren," said Lincoln, ignoring the reality of the Civil War. The President spoke slowly and paused frequently, allowing Smith ample time to translate. The Indians must have liked what they heard, because they responded "with frequent marks of applause and approbation . . . and their countenances gave evident tokens of satisfaction," one witness observed.

After the brief ceremony, Lincoln moved along the line of delegates, shaking hands and chatting with each one, including the two women, who shook his hand vigorously and with every expression of delight. "Those girls," commented one observer, "will go home highly elated by the honor thus unexpectedly conferred upon them, and will probably boast all their days that they shook hands with the great Chief of the Palefaces." Finally, in a White House ceremony that included the pomp and formalities accorded visiting heads of state, Lincoln exchanged gifts with the delegates and hosted an informal reception featuring wine, cake, and other refreshments.

As soon as Lincoln left the circle, the crowd pressed in closer to the Indians, marveling at their dress and pestering them with questions, which the interpreter patiently tried to translate. Yellow Wolf of the Kiowa expressed enthusiasm at meeting the President. His warmth quickly made him the favorite of the spectators, who were overheard saying things like, "He is a good fellow," and "There, now, I like that one."

Before leaving, the Indians posed for photographs in the conservatory. Nicolay later sent one to a friend. "A delegation of Indians from the plains were here to see the President, and afterwards they were taken out to the greenhouse and photographed," he wrote in an accompanying note. "I have a stereoscopic view of it which shows to better advantage."

*F*ollowing a routine developed decades earlier, the Indian delegates made the usual rounds of government offices and churches. Since Commissioner Dole had been unable to obtain passes to visit military installations, the delegates went to the theater instead. On the evening of March 30, they saw the new romantic play *St. Marc, or the Soldier of Fortune* at Grover's Theater on Pennsylvania Avenue. Knowing of their plans in advance, the *Morning Chronicle* encouraged theatergoers to attend, assuring that they would be able to see these "representatives of the influential tribes in the West—all great fighting nations—in their peculiar paints, [and] costumes." The Indians were obviously as much of an attraction as the play itself. Newspapers even reported their seating arrangements. Crowds besieged them everywhere. Five Washington and New York newspapers covered the meeting with Lincoln, and stories about their activities appeared in newspapers as far away as California. Noah Brooks of the *Sacramento Union* wrote, for example, that while most of the visiting chiefs dressed in their native finery, some of the party had been "coaxed into hiding their nakedness in the dingy garments of civilization, in which they looked about as comfortable as bears in moccasins."

The members of the 1863 Southern Plains delegation received the Abraham Lincoln peace medal (opposite). Its reverse side bore a confused design, with one Indian wearing a war bonnet while plowing his fields and another Indian scalping a fallen enemy.

Expected to remain in the East for several weeks, the delegates' stay was cut short by the death of Yellow Wolf, who came down with pneumonia days after he met Lincoln. Washington delegations always involved a long and arduous journey for these tribal elders, and a number of chiefs died en route or in Washington, some of smallpox, many of pneumonia. Thirty-some chiefs are buried in Washington area cemeteries. Yellow Wolf died a week after he fell sick and, like everything else about the delegation, his illness and funeral received extensive press coverage. Even his dying words appeared in the newspapers.

"Tell my people that I entreat them with my last breath to live in peace with the pale faces," Yellow Wolf was reported to have said as he clasped Colley's hand. "Tell them that I have seen their 'Great Father,' and that he has promised to take care of the red man. . . . I have ever been a friend to the pale face, and the inheritance I would leave to my nation is that they conduct themselves so as to merit the smile of the Great Spirit, which watches over the red man and the pale face."

Yellow Wolf was buried in Washington's Congressional Cemetery, joining the famous Choctaw chief Pushmataha and a score of other Indians who had died while visiting the Great Father. He was given a proper Christian burial—in the eyes of U.S. officials, yet another learning experience for his fellow delegates. The other delegates prepared Yellow Wolf's body for burial, garbing him in his finest clothing and ceremonial paint, breaking his bow and arrows in half and placing them in his coffin, along with other objects—including the Thomas Jefferson peace medal, passed down through generations, which he had proudly brought to Washington, declaring it one of his tribe's most prized possessions.

That medal could have been one of those carried by Lewis and Clark or Zebulon Pike on their westward travels. Many believed the rare object should go to the Smithsonian Institution. To bury the medal "appears almost ridiculous," one reporter complained, "as it has been handed down from father to son since the days of J[efferson], and is a connective link between the present and the past and should be placed in charge of the government. But the Indians insist upon its interment with Yellow Wolf, and the Agents do not desire to offend them by a refusal."

After Yellow Wolf's death, the Indians of the 1863 delegation were anxious to return home, but first they had to endure a visit to New York City, where the consummate entertainer, P. T. Barnum—who had bribed Colley with "a pretty liberal outlay of money"—displayed them. The delegates paraded through the streets of New York on a circus wagon and stood on stage while Barnum spoke in words they did not understand, perpetuating the stereotypes of scoundrel, rapist, and warmonger.

About the only difficulty Barnum had with the arrangement was the Indians' desire for curiosities from his museum. A shirt of chain mail attracted particular attention. Barnum did not want to part with the popular attraction, but the delegates were so insistent on having it that he finally traded it to a Kiowa chief for a suit of buckskins. A decade later, a Kiowa warrior wearing a chain mail shirt was killed at the Battle of Adobe Walls in eastern Texas.

Other than providing Washington a welcome diversion from the Civil War, the delegation of 1863 accomplished nothing. A treaty of friendship with the Comanche and Kiowa was proposed, but the Senate—so much more concerned about the solidarity of the Union—tabled it. The threat of Indian uprisings in the West continued, a constant irritant in the minds of government officials but nothing deserving of the same attention as the War between the States. In fact, when Little Wolf returned from Washington, he told his people that "the whites are all at war in the states and that they will all kill one another and the Indians will be able to take [back] this country in [the] spring." ↵

Pennsylvania artist George Catlin roamed the West during the 1830s in a relentless search for Indian scenes. He created this double portrait of The Light, an Assiniboin chief, before and after his 1832 Washington visit. Catlin portrayed The Light in a military greatcoat, hiding whiskey bottles. Tribesmen disconcerted by his new ways killed The Light soon after he went home to the Northern Plains.

DELEGATIONS TO WASHINGTON

✳

*T*he plan to invite tribal leaders to visit the nation's capital as guests of the United States government was a cornerstone of American Indian policy that reached from the 18th century and the founding of the Republic into the 20th century. Each delegation followed a similar script. The chiefs received guided tours of arsenals, battleships, and forts; endured the attention of press and public as they attended theatrical performances, art galleries, and other cultural offerings; and met with a variety of government officials, often even the President of the United States, whom they called the "Great Father"—never the "Great White Father," a fiction invented by the dime-novel industry.

The delegates usually stayed for several weeks, housed in one of the better hotels along Pennsylvania Avenue. During their stay many gifts, including new clothing, were showered upon them. Indeed the first appointments on their busy schedules were visits to tailor shops and department stores, so that the delegation Indians could be fitted with the latest sartorial fashions.

Visits to photography studios were also always on the schedule: Delegation photographs were popular items in those days. Photographers were especially anxious to shoot photographs of the chiefs before they changed into their newly purchased wardrobes. If the chiefs arrived at the studio without their own weapons, the photographers had props on hand to make the stereotype complete.

Indians in war bonnets were commercially valuable. These Yankton Sioux, visiting Washington from South Dakota, part of a 1905 delegation, may have thought they were getting a city tour—but they were helping to promote the new Toledo Touring Car.

In this earliest known photograph of Indians in Washington (and very likely the earliest of the White House), members of four 1857 delegations stand in front of the South Portico. Delegates represented tribes from the Central Plains: Pawnee, Ponca, Sac and Fox, and Potawatomi. The photograph was probably commissioned for the Illustrated London News.

In 1880 these Jicarilla Apache delegates from the New Mexico Territory— from left to right, Santiago Largo, Guerito, Augustine Vigil, San Pablo, and Juan Julian—visited the Corcoran Gallery of Art and posed in front of "The Passing Regiment" by Jean Baptiste Edouard Detaille and "Niagara" by Frederic Edwin Church.

the Sand Creek Massacre

"*A number of us mounted our horses
and followed Lean Bear, our chief,
out to meet the soldiers . . .
We did not want to fight.*"

—WOLF CHIEF, REMEMBERING THE MURDER OF LEAN BEAR

Once one of North America's most abundant animal species, the American bison suffered a dramatic decline in the 19th century. William F. "Buffalo Bill" Cody claimed he bagged 4,280 buffalo in 18 months and once killed 48 in 50 minutes.

1864

✳

ome in the Southern Plains after their lengthy trip east, perhaps even hopeful for peace between the white man and their people, Lean Bear and the other Cheyenne and Arapaho leaders began to sense increasing unrest. Militant young men were threatening more harm to intruding whites. Hunger and death were stalking their villages. The buffalo were disappearing: That winter agent Colley reported that none were to be found within 200 miles of the reservation established by the Treaty of Fort Wise. Small game was equally scarce. Colley admitted that the Indians under his jurisdiction were harassing wagon trains and white outposts, but they were seeking food, not scalps. "Most of the depredations committed by them are from starvation," he wrote. "It is hard for them to understand that they have no right to take from them that have, when in a starving condition."

No matter. Colorado authorities had been seeking a pretext to justify a war against the Indians. Governor John Evans, for one, had hoped for a rationale since his first days in office. People moving into the territory, hungry for gold and silver, just wanted the Indians out of their way.

The problem was a lack of hostile Indians to fight. Rumors of Indian raids sent troops rushing in all directions. They seldom encountered hostiles, but they did contribute to the general hysteria. By attacking and killing any luckless Indians they encountered, the soldiers stirred up the war spirit of tribal peoples otherwise inclined to remain at peace.

Typical were the exploits of Lt. George S. Eayre, sent in search of 200 head of cattle that some Cheyenne Indians purportedly stole from a government contractor. With 50 troopers and two howitzers, Eayre headed east into Kansas, where he found an abandoned village whose occupants had obviously fled, having learned of his coming. Eayre's troops burned the lodges, all the gear and equipment in the camp, and piles of dried buffalo meat. Another village 15 miles farther away suffered the same treatment.

PRECEDING PAGES: In 1936, artist Robert Lindneux painted the scene of the 1864 U.S. Army attack on Black Kettle's village in eastern Colorado Territory, known to history as the Sand Creek Massacre.

The railroads invited white sportsmen to experience the thrill of killing buffalo from their trains. The Kansas Pacific Railway operated its own taxidermy shop, advertising with this photograph of elk horns and buffalo heads outside the general railway offices in Kansas City.

Eayre returned to Denver for supplies and additional men, then went back to Kansas with orders, according to one of his troopers, "to kill Cheyennes whenever and wherever found." On May 16, he stumbled on another settlement. Four hundred Cheyenne and Arapaho occupied this village, including Lean Bear, the chief who had met Lincoln, and Black Kettle, another chief who sought peaceful coexistence. In fact, Black Kettle's name headed the list of those who had signed the 1861 Fort Wise Treaty, accepting a reservation in exchange for lands identified as theirs in an agreement signed ten years before.

The Indians in the village were traveling north, seeking buffalo. They had no reason to anticipate the violence about to engulf them. They were camped near Ash Creek when a crier raced through the village, announcing soldiers with cannons. "A number of us mounted our horses and followed Lean Bear, our chief, out to meet the soldiers," Wolf Chief, then in the village, later told historian George Bird Grinnell. "We did not want to fight." The warriors approached and saw soldiers in formation. "Lean Bear told us to stay behind him while he went forward to show his papers from Washington, which would tell the soldiers we were friendly," Wolf Chief recalled.

Lean Bear, accompanied by his son, Star, came forward, waving a sheet of paper in his hand. When the officer saw him approaching, he shouted out an order. Soldiers opened fire, knocking Lean Bear and Star off their ponies. The soldiers galloped forward and shot the fallen Indians again. When soldiers examined Lean Bear's body, his Lincoln peace medal still hung around his neck, and his hand still clutched a letter on U.S. government stationery. It read:

Col. John M. Chivington was zealously pursuing a political career when he attacked Black Kettle's village. The brutal massacre did nothing for his political ambitions. He returned to Ohio and died in obscurity.

> *This is to certify that Lean Bear, a member of the Cheyenne tribe of Indians in Colorado Territory, has visited the city of Washington on business connected with the interests of his tribe, and while in that city he has behaved himself in an orderly and peaceful manner. He has promised his Great Father always to be friendly towards the white men, and never again molest them while passing through his country; and any white man to whom he may show this paper, is requested by the Government to behave towards him in a friendly manner, and to be very careful not to give him any cause to break his promises to his Great Father.*

SIGNED: WILLIAM P. DOLE,
COMMISSIONER OF INDIAN AFFAIRS

Lean Bear's assassination sparked a brief but spirited battle. The soldiers blasted away with grape shot and the Indians returned fire, killing several. Finally Black Kettle rode out from the village. "He told us we must not fight the white people, so we stopped," Wolf Chief said. The soldiers retreated. Twenty-eight Cheyenne lay dead.

Governor Evans now had his Indian war. Sporadic fighting kept breaking out across the territory, creating a frenzy in white communities fed by sensational newspaper accounts of alleged Indian atrocities. Governor Evans warned Washington that Indian hordes were about to destroy Colorado communities.

It was in this electrified atmosphere that military leaders in Washington, preoccupied with their own war, authorized Evans to establish a short-lived cavalry regiment, the Third Colorado, giving it only a hundred days in which to get the job done. Local men, many confirmed Indian haters already, volunteered. Their commander was John M. Chivington, a former Methodist clergyman dubbed the "Fighting

FOLLOWING PAGES: The buffalo was the lifeblood of the Plains Indians, physically and spiritually, providing food, clothing, shelter, blankets, tools, ornaments, and campfire fuel.

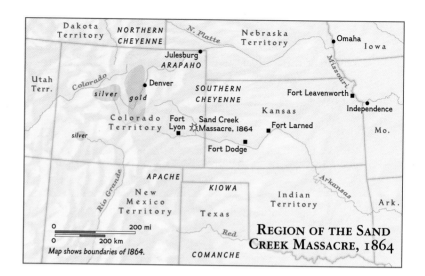

Parson" for his exploits against Confederate forces in New Mexico. A man of enormous ego and ambition, Chivington welcomed the opportunity. As the regiment took shape, though, the emergency evaporated. The anger among the various tribes had eased, and most of the regiment's intended targets had slipped back home to prepare for winter.

Meanwhile Black Kettle, hoping to calm matters even more, had written a letter seeking peace and offering to surrender white prisoners held by some of his people. The letter was received by Maj. Edward W. Wynkoop, commander of Fort Lyon. Compassionate and open-minded, Wynkoop was a rarity in that charged climate. He met with Black Kettle, received four white prisoners, and promised a peaceful solution to the crisis.

But that was not the goal of either Governor Evans or the U.S. Army. "I want no peace till the Indians suffer more," telegraphed Gen. Samuel R. Curtis, Chivington's superior officer, from Fort Leavenworth. Governor Evans was also in a quandary. He had recently campaigned for Colorado to attain statehood. Watching his bid voted down, he was even more sensitive over the prospect of losing face if no Indians were punished during the enlistments of the "Hundred Dazers."

*M*eanwhile Cheyenne and Arapaho leaders, including Black Kettle and Little Raven, willingly traveled under Army escort to talk peace with U.S. officials. They did not want to be seen as hostiles. Told to go and surrender to Major Wynkoop, Little Raven immediately led the people of his village to Fort Lyon, arriving in mid-October. Black Kettle arrived in early November, although he left the people of his village, camping in some 115 lodges, at Sand Creek, about 35 miles northeast of Fort Lyon.

Arriving at the fort, these Indians did not get the response they anticipated. Major Wynkoop had been summoned east to explain to General Curtis why presumably hostile Indians were being welcomed by the Army. Moreover, Wynkoop had insufficient rations to feed so many Indians, and he needed authorization to accept them as prisoners. Little Raven and the Arapaho were advised to move away from the fort so they could better hunt for food. Black Kettle was told to remain at Sand Creek, where there was game to hunt.

At the same time, Chivington was feeling the pressure to perform. He and his hundred-day volunteers were being ridiculed by the Colorado press, who called them the "Bloodless Third" because they had not shot a single hostile. Their hundred days were about to expire, and if any Indian fighting was to be done, it had to be done soon. But the only Indians within easy reach were in Black Kettle's village, camped on Sand Creek. Even though Black Kettle had followed government orders and come to Fort Lyon, then obediently returned to Sand Creek, Chivington rationalized, he and his villagers had not officially surrendered. Some of the warriors in the village were doubtless guilty of harassing whites in the territory—so Chivington justified taking matters into his own hands, and he sent his cavalry into action.

On November 28, 1864, under cover of darkness, the Third

Major Wynkoop, left, and Colonel Chivington squat for a photograph during their September 1864 meeting with Black Kettle, seated just behind Wynkoop. Standing behind Black Kettle is interpreter John S. Smith, who witnessed the Sand Creek Massacre.

FOLLOWING PAGES: Wild asters paint the summer Flint Hills of Kansas a dappled purple. In the 1860s, this idyllic landscape was home to the Cheyenne and Arapaho Indians.

Lakota Sioux at the Pine Ridge Reservation in Dakota Territory wait in line for food allotments from the government on ration day. Intended to ease the transition

from hunting to farming, the program was a failure. At left, Comanche women and
children pose glumly for a photograph at Fort Sill in Oklahoma.

"When we see the soldiers
moving away
and the forts abandoned
then I will come down
and talk."

— RED CLOUD, INVITED TO SIGN
THE FORT LARAMIE TREATY

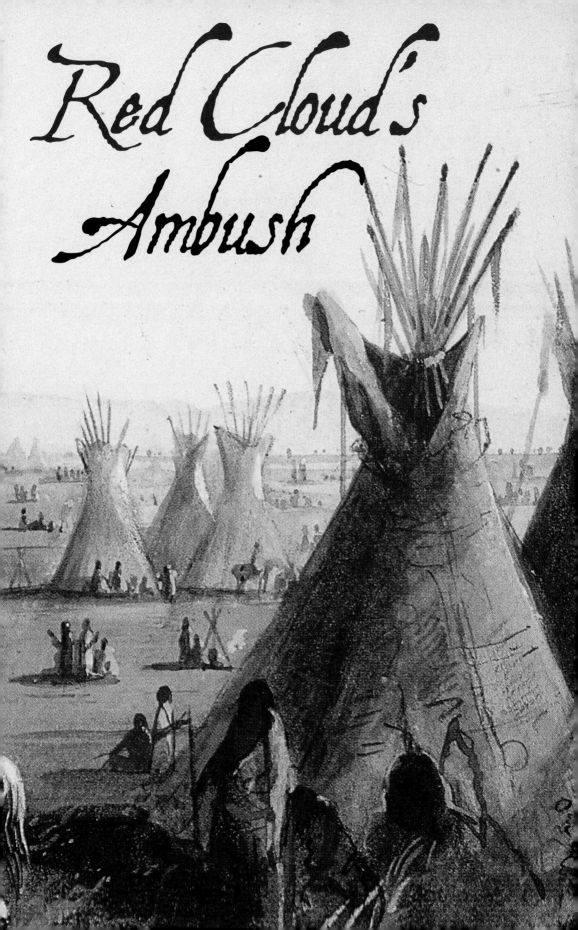

Red Cloud's Ambush

In 1868 Gen. William Tecumseh Sherman, silhouetted among the commissioners, met Sioux leaders, seated at left, to negotiate use of the lands of the Northern Plains.

1866

✳

The massacre perpetrated by Chivington's Third on Black Kettle and his people riled up tribes across the Plains. Increased Indian belligerence gave soldiers ample opportunity to put their fighting skills to the test. Army leaders felt confident that their men, the same soldiers who had defeated the Confederacy, could easily quell any Indian unrest. At the same time Western settlers scorned any government policy that appeared soft on Indians. Few Westerners took Indian likes and dislikes seriously. Official policies and everyday practices developed entirely for the sake of the white population, without any regard for the culture, habits, needs, or preferences of the resident Indian tribes. Graffiti found scrawled on an Indian skull—"I am on the reservation at last"—expressed the destiny most Westerners envisioned for the Indians.

In January and February of 1865, Cheyenne and Arapaho war parties burned ranches and plundered wagon trains in Colorado. They cut telegraph wires going into Denver and twice terrorized the town of Julesburg, running off livestock, looting buildings, and killing stragglers. One war party, trying to block train tracks with a log, derailed a steam engine used by construction crews building the transcontinental railroad. Southern Cheyenne still tell the story of a luckless telegraph operator killed in one of their raids. Aware that white people somehow talked over the wire, warriors shoved telegraph wire through the operator's head from ear to ear "so he could hear better in the afterlife."

The soldier assigned to the problem was Gen. John Pope, whose brutal treatment of the Santee Sioux in Minnesota in 1862 had won favor from Westerners and military superiors. Now, in the spring of 1865, in command of most of the western theater and convinced that all Plains tribes were hostile, Pope hurled 6,000 combat troops in three armies against the Comanche and Kiowa on the Southern Plains and against the Arapaho, Cheyenne, and Sioux on the Central and Northern Plains.

Other than to anger the Indians and embarrass the Army, Pope's campaign accomplished nothing except to provide a valuable military

PRECEDING PAGES: *Albert Jacob Miller's 1837 painting depicts an Indian encampment in the Dakota Territory.*

lesson: Feeding and supporting the unwieldy Army columns absorbed so much time and energy, there was little left with which to pursue Indians. Inhospitable weather further hampered military effectiveness. One unit not only lost most of its horses and mules to early winter storms but came perilously close to losing its personnel as well.

A peace of sorts was achieved—temporarily, and not through force of arms. The general population of the United States, horrified by the atrocities at Sand Creek, wanted the bloodshed to stop. Before Pope's troops returned from the field, government officials were already extending olive branches to the militant tribes, asking them to assemble at Fort Laramie in the Dakota Territory, today's Wyoming, in the spring of 1866, to establish "a lasting peace" on the Northern Plains.

When news went out that government officials wished to talk of peace and were promising presents and badly needed food, several thousand Sioux and Cheyenne gathered at Fort Laramie to meet with the Great Father's representatives. E. B. Taylor led the government contingent. Foremost among the militant Indians was Red Cloud, the Oglala war chief whose name, along with those of Crazy Horse and Sitting Bull, was to become a household word in the coming decades.

The government did not wish to purchase their country, officials told the Indians. It simply wanted to make peace and obtain permission for white travelers to use the Bozeman Trail, a new road through the Powder River country that linked the Oregon Trail with the Montana gold fields. They promised that all travelers would stay on the Bozeman Trail and would not hunt—a promise that was, one official later admitted, "well calculated, and . . . designed to deceive."

*R*ed Cloud was not fooled. Travelers were already using the road. When Col. Henry B. Carrington and his infantry marched into Fort Laramie amidst the proceedings, the Oglala chief suspected what was going on. In fact, Carrington already had orders to build a string of posts along the Bozeman Trail. At the conference, Red Cloud refused the Army colonel an introduction and, according to witnesses, rebuked him for being a party to deceit: "The Great Father sends us presents and wants us to sell him the road, but the White Chief goes with soldiers to steal the road before the Indians say yes or no!" With that, Red Cloud stalked away, taking most of the militant Indians with him.

Commissioner Taylor continued with the conference nonetheless and persuaded the remaining chiefs to sign the treaty and agree that white

By taking an uncompromising stand against white encroachment, Red Cloud, the Oglala Sioux chief, fired the fighting spirit of the Northern Plains tribes. A unique individual possessed of notable political and military skills, to Easterners Red Cloud epitomized the concept of the noble red man.

settlers could use the Bozeman Trail. He did not seem concerned that the signatories were primarily "Laramie Loafers"—friendly Indians who spent most of their time lounging around the fort—and a handful of leaders whose tribes would not be affected by the proposed right-of-way. "Satisfactory treaty concluded with the Sioux and Cheyennes," Taylor immediately wired Washington. "Most cordial feelings prevail."

The true extent of those cordial feelings soon became evident. Red Cloud's war parties harassed both travelers and garrisons building the three Bozeman Trail forts: Fort C. F. Smith, Fort Reno, and Fort Phil Kearney, the primary post and Carrington's headquarters. Around Fort Phil Kearney, Carrington decided to erect a log palisade, a defensive perimeter seldom seen in forts west of the Mississippi.

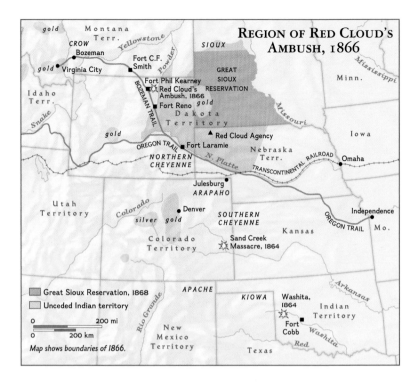

Red Cloud continually sent out war parties against work crews who were cutting trees on the slopes of nearby mountains. He also attacked the train bringing logs to the fort—an endeavor that gave him his finest moment and also enabled a bold young Sioux warrior named Crazy Horse to join the pantheon of American Indian heroes.

On a brisk winter day in December 1866, a war party attacked the wood train within sight of the fort. Carrington sent Capt. William J. Fetterman and a combined force of 2 civilians and 79 cavalry and infantrymen to chase them away. Fetterman was a brash and foolhardy Civil War veteran who ridiculed the fighting abilities of the Plains Indians. Only days before, he had boasted that he could march through the entire Sioux nation with only 80 men. With Fetterman was Capt. Frederick Brown, regimental quartermaster, who had just been promoted and ordered east. Brown craved another Indian battle before he left, and as the column was about to leave the fort, he appealed to Carrington "for one more chance to bring in the scalp of Red Cloud himself."

Colonel Carrington knew better than to send a handful of troops into battle against an unseen foe. He sprang to the sentry walk on the stockade and shouted, "Support the wood train, relieve it, and report

RED CLOUD'S AMBUSH

to me. . . . Under no circumstances pursue over Lodge Trail Ridge." Fetterman ignored those orders. He and his little command pursued the party that had attacked the train—a small band, led by a warrior whose pony appeared to be limping badly.

That warrior was Crazy Horse, who played his role to perfection. A fearless, modest, slightly built young man, one of the Oglala tribe of the Lakota Sioux, Crazy Horse entered history with this bold tactic, which led to the demise of Fetterman and his unfortunate troopers. According to He Dog, another noted Oglala military leader, "Crazy Horse always led his men himself when they went into battle, and he kept well in front of them. He headed many charges." This time he led warriors in an apparent retreat over the Lodge Trail Ridge. U.S. troops chased after him—and fell into the hands of some 2,000 Sioux, Arapaho, and Cheyenne warriors.

The decoy strategy was the favorite of the Plains Indians. A few hand-picked warriors, serving as decoys, revealed themselves to a numerically superior enemy force and then slowly retreated, hoping that the enemy would follow them into an ambush. The tactic almost never worked because young warriors lying in ambush seldom had the patience

The sun sets over the hills near the Washita River, in today's Oklahoma, where in 1868 Lt. Col. George Armstrong Custer and the Seventh Cavalry killed the Cheyenne chief Black Kettle and destroyed his unsuspecting village in an operation that came to be known as the Battle of the Washita.

to wait for the enemy to enter the trap before attacking. But this time the strategy worked perfectly. The huge Indian force waited until all of Fetterman's men had come over the ridge and out of sight of the fort.

The soldiers never had a chance. "When the charge was made," recalled White Elk, a Cheyenne warrior who told his story a half century later, "the sound of many hoofs made a noise like thunder." The first to die were the foot soldiers, the last to come over the ridge. The cavalry, under Lt. George Grummond, was at the bottom of the ridge, a mile or so ahead of the infantry, when the attack began. They tried to spur their horses back up the ridge but never made it. "The arrows flew so thickly above the troops that they seemed like a lot of grasshoppers flying across each other," White Elk remembered. "Soon the ground was so thickly covered with arrows, a man had only to reach down and pick up one that had landed next to him."

Warriors, too, were hit by the flying arrows. White Elk saw a Lakota die instantly when an arrow pierced his forehead. Another Lakota took an arrow in the shoulder. Meanwhile, some of the cavalrymen managed to dismount and hide among huge rocks below the crest of the ridge. Rather than risk a frontal assault, the warriors surrounded the rocks and crept forward, yelling encouragement and directions to each other.

"Get ready!" someone would yell. "We are ready," others would respond. Finally, a chief yelled "Charge!" Warriors sprinted in from all sides. Several Sioux died in the hand-to-hand fighting. Three or four soldiers shot themselves, fearful of being captured alive.

In a moment it was over. Only a dog that had followed the troops from Fort Phil Kearney remained. "All are dead but the dog," someone yelled. "Let him carry the news to the fort."

"No," shouted Big Rascal, a Cheyenne. "Do not let even a dog get away!" With that, an arrow struck and killed the dog.

*F*rom the condition of the horribly mutilated bodies left behind after the ambush, it was obvious that Red Cloud's warriors intended to make a statement. One corpse, that of a civilian who joined the column to test his new repeating rifle, had 105 arrows in it.

The body of bugler Adolph Metzger was not mutilated. A career soldier and veteran of the Civil War, he had fought bravely, using his bugle as a club, and the Indians respectfully covered him and his bugle with a buffalo robe. Captains Fetterman and Brown were found lying next to each other among the rocks. Evidently terrified at the prospect of being captured alive, they had committed suicide by shooting each other in the head. Indian fatalities numbered 14, according to Two Moons, a Cheyenne chief: 11 Sioux, 2 Cheyenne, and 1 Arapaho.

Red Cloud's stunning victory brought immediate and surprising results. The Army, of course, demanded revenge—or, at the very least, responsibility for Indian affairs, which they wanted transferred from the Department of the Interior to the War Department. Federal bureaucrats had coddled Indians long enough. Gen. William Tecumseh Sherman—the Union hero famous for his ruthless marches through Atlanta and the farmlands of the South—now commanded all Federal troops on the Great Plains, declaring, "We must act with vindictive earnestness . . . even to their extermination—men, women, and children."

President Andrew Johnson had other ideas. Heeding the advice of James R. Doolittle, chairman of the Senate Committee on Indian Affairs, Johnson and his administration sought a peaceful resolution to the Indian problem. In 1867, a peace commission toured the Plains and concluded that whites had provoked most instances of Indian violence. The commission recommended two large Indian reserves, one for the Northern Plains tribes, the other for the Southern Plains tribes. Between them, north of the Platte River and south of the Arkansas, the United States would establish a broad thoroughfare to the West, over which emigrant trains and the transcontinental railroad could pass unmolested.

Accordingly, in 1868, treaty commissioners again met at Fort Laramie, seeking approval from the Northern Plains tribes to establish a large reservation north of Nebraska and west of the Missouri River. In return, the government promised to abandon the forts on the Bozeman Trail and to close the Powder River country to all whites, deeming it "unceded Indian territory." A number of Sioux leaders signed the treaty, but none representing the hostile bands. As for Red Cloud, he sent a firm message that dictated his terms: "We are on the mountains looking down on the soldiers and forts. When we see the soldiers moving away and the forts abandoned then I will come down and talk."

At the end of July, the troops marched away. Only then, after his warriors had reduced the hated forts to cinders, did Red Cloud add his signature to the Fort Laramie Treaty. This marks one of the few occasions when the white man retreated, but some scholars now believe that monied interests orchestrated the entire episode in order to distract Red Cloud and his warriors from construction sites along the transcontinental railroad, soon to make trails such as the Bozeman obsolete anyway.

For Red Cloud and the Sioux, it was a symbolic victory at best. The 1868 Fort Laramie Treaty did cede rights to the territory covered

FOLLOWING PAGES: The Bozeman Trail departed from the main wagon road and led to the Montana gold fields. Established by John Bozeman, who later died at Indian hands on the trail, it sliced through some of the best hunting grounds of the Northern Plains Indians.

RED CLOUD

✳

Chief Red Cloud of the Oglala Sioux was the preeminent tribal leader of his day. At once a warrior, a statesman, and a politician, he was shrewd, intelligent, and resourceful. Entering the national stage at a time of crisis for the tribes of the Northern Plains, he established a strong Indian coalition that delayed the relentless westward march of the United States by forcing the close of the Bozeman Trail. Government leaders took seriously the wishes of this formidable Sioux adversary.

Born in 1822 near what is now North Platte, Nebraska, Red Cloud spent much of his early life at war—against traditional tribal enemies and then against the United States, culminating in the destruction of Capt. William Fetterman's command in 1866. When he signed the Fort Laramie Treaty two years later, Red Cloud gave up his warrior ways and launched his equally successful career as a statesman and political leader.

He visited leaders in the East, including the President of the United States, at least 12 times over the next 30 years, lobbying for the preservation of Indian lands, Indian rights, and tribal sovereignty. Always regal in bearing and demeanor, he epitomized the noble red man to eastern reformers and humanitarians, who took great satisfaction when he changed his name to John Red Cloud and converted to Christianity before his death in 1909.

Chief Red Cloud, opposite right, and Little Wound traveled to Washington as part of the Oglala Sioux delegation of 1880. Behind them is their interpreter, John Bridgeman.

This photograph of Red Cloud wearing fashionable attire is undated but was probably taken during the chief's May 1880 visit to the Carlisle Indian Industrial School.

Near 90 and blind, Red Cloud died in 1909. His long, complex life as a warrior, diplomat, and lobbyist testifies to the many ways American Indians resisted conquest.

"Tell 'Washington' to give us our women and children and send us to a country where we can work and live like white men."

— Mamanti, a Kiowa chief imprisoned at Fort Marion

the Fort Marion Experience

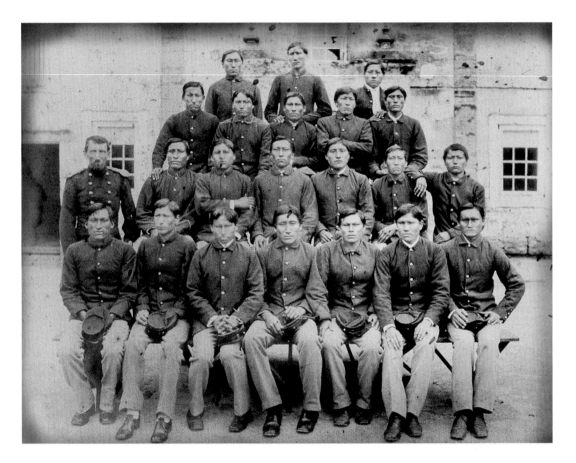

Male Indians of the Southern Plains identified as hostile were rounded up and sent to Fort Marion, Florida, under the guardianship of Capt. Richard Henry Pratt, standing far left. This group posed in uniform a few days before their release in 1878.

1875

✴

In the spring of 1874, pent-up frustrations over unfulfilled promises and the wanton slaughter of buffalo by hide hunters exploded into the Red River War: the last desperate but hopeless resistance by Southern Plains tribes to the new order. From encampments deep in the country surrounding the headwaters of the Washita and the forks of the Red River, Arapaho, Comanche, Kiowa, and Cheyenne young men went seeking revenge for real and imagined wrongs.

The warriors targeted buffalo hunters. They surprised two dozen hunters at a camp at Adobe Walls, a makeshift trading post in the Texas Panhandle, but well-armed marksmen repelled the attack. Less fortunate farm families fell victim to the angry tribesmen.

The attacks provoked a prompt and aggressive response from government officials and red-faced Army officers who had claimed that Indian wars on the Southern Plains were over. Cavalry patrols, often aided by tribal members in the Army's employ, scoured the Plains in search of the hostiles. With the buffalo all but gone and soldiers at every turn, the war chiefs had no alternative but to surrender. One by one, the militants turned in their guns and returned to the agencies. By the spring of 1875, the Red River War was over.

Determined to end Indian belligerency on the Southern Plains once and for all, the U.S. government decided upon a draconian policy: All warriors found guilty of crimes during the outbreak were to be arrested and jailed far from home. Chiefs who fingered troublemakers among their followers would be guaranteed immunity from punishment.

The upshot of this policy was that individuals were proclaimed guilty in arbitrary and capricious ways. At the Darlington Agency in Oklahoma, headquarters for the Southern Cheyenne and Arapaho, a drunken Army officer lined up all the recently surrendered Cheyenne warriors. He haphazardly identified a dozen or so men and claimed them guilty of specific crimes. Then, to quicken his task, he directed that the 18 Indians standing at the right of the line join the group proclaimed

PRECEDING PAGES: *The Indians imprisoned at Fort Marion were encouraged to draw. Zotom, a Kiowa, drew this scene of the prisoners after their arrival.*

guilty. He promised to examine them more carefully at a later time—but never did.

Among that group was Black Horse, a young warrior whose great-grandson, Ben Nighthorse Campbell, would win election to the U.S. Senate from Colorado in 1992. Black Horse was accused of being a "ringleader"—a vague term which meant no specific charge could be found against him. Guilty or not, on April 6, 1875, he and the other Cheyenne prisoners were taken to the agency blacksmith to be fitted with balls and chains. As they waited in line for their irons, Cheyenne women watched the public humiliation of their loved ones and began singing battle songs to lift their spirits.

This was all the encouragement Black Horse needed. As the black-smith leaned over to fit the bracelet around his ankle, Black Horse kicked him in the chin. He dashed toward tepees on the other side of a nearby creek—and never made it. The guards, caught by surprise, recovered quickly and fired a barrage of bullets. One caught Black Horse in the side and knocked him off his feet.

Within minutes a state of war existed at Darlington. Some 200 Cheyenne—men, women, and children—rushed to nearby sand hills to dig trenches and recover guns and ammunition they had hidden there for just such an emergency. During the confusion, several men still waiting to be ironed rushed over, picked up Black Horse, and carried him to safety.

For the rest of the day and well into the evening, a terrific battle ensued. The Cheyenne refused to surrender, even though the Army blazed away with a Gatling gun to dislodge the frightened Indians from their trenches. During the night, as the Army prepared for an all-out assault at dawn, the Cheyenne slipped away. Many eventually returned to the agency, but others decided to join their northern relatives. Among those heading north was Black Horse. Although officially counted among the dead that day, he recovered fully from his wound and eventually found his way to Montana, where he continued in the struggles of his people.

*N*ot all captured were so lucky. Despite the resistance at Darlington, 74 Indians were rounded up and sent east. Fort Sill, agency head-quarters for the Comanche and Kiowa, reported sending 27 Kiowa, 11 Comanche, and 1 Caddo (who had been accused of murdering another Caddo). Darlington sent 2 Arapaho and 33 Cheyenne (32 men and 1 woman, who had killed a white farmer with an axe). Some of the

More than half of the Fort Marion prisoners made pictographs. Zotom compiled a pictographic diary that documents his transition from warrior to prisoner to student. This drawing shows the prisoners assembling to leave Fort Sill—a tense moment made all the more so by women and children who wailed and cried as they helplessly watched their loved ones being taken away.

Leaving Ft Sill for Florida

prisoners had indeed committed atrocities, but most were ordinary young men guilty of no more than leading the traditional life of a Plains Indian warrior. To their white neighbors, for example, stealing horses was a major crime against society. But to them it was a great achievement: a coup. To a young warrior, counting coup, or accumulating such war honors, was akin to youngsters in our society earning merit badges toward the rank of Eagle Scout. Of the prisoners identified as Kiowa and Comanche, 11 were actually Mexicans who had been captured as children and raised as Indians. Also in the party were Maltur, a Comanche mother, and her eight-year-old daughter. Maltur had clung to her husband so tightly that the Army officer felt he had only two choices: to shoot her or to let her come along. He simply shrugged his shoulders and put her in the wagon, saying, "Let someone else down the line deal with this."

Among the prisoners were a few leaders: Black Horse, a Comanche (not the Cheyenne leader); Gray Beard, Minimic, Heap of Birds, and Medicine Water, all Cheyenne; and White Horse, Mamanti, Woman's Heart, and Lone Wolf of the Kiowa. The government claimed that their tribes

FOLLOWING PAGES:
Emotions ran high as the prisoners passed by scenes such as this sunset, traveling east to an unknown destination.

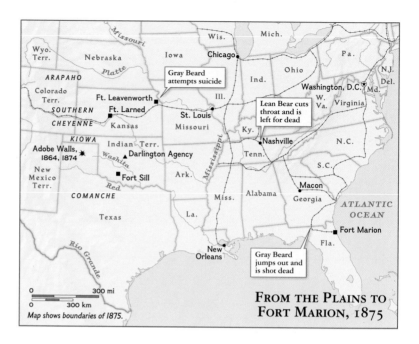

FROM THE PLAINS TO FORT MARION, 1875

Map shows boundaries of 1875.

would adjust more easily to reservation life without the disruptive presence of former war leaders. In fact, the prisoners were hostages taken to ensure the good behavior of their kinsmen at home. Perhaps the most notable was Lone Wolf, who had by then traveled to Washington with two delegations, the one in 1863 and another in 1872. Apparently they had done little to make him want to embrace the white man's road.

The prisoners assembled at Fort Sill were shipped east to Fort Marion, in St. Augustine, Florida, a dank fortress on the Atlantic seacoast. Today a national monument, this 17th-century Spanish fort was the government's 19th-century prison of choice for Indians deemed hostile by U.S. authorities. Assigned to escort them to Florida was Richard Henry Pratt, an Army captain and humanitarian whose name was to become synonymous with Indian education.

Pratt had fought as a second lieutenant during the Civil War. After that, he led the Tenth Cavalry, a black regiment, on duty in the Southern Plains, aided by a corps of Indian scouts. By the time of the Fort Marion assignment, he had spent the better part of a decade fighting the Comanche, Kiowa, Cheyenne, and Arapaho.

Originally, Pratt was only to escort the prisoners to Fort Leavenworth, in Kansas, but he offered to take them all the way to Florida if he could visit his family in the East after the journey. "I want to go," he admitted, "because I have been on duty in the Indian Territory eight years and desire a change." The Army granted his request, thereby allowing him to begin conceiving his remarkably unique approach to Indian education.

The journey took 24 days. The prisoners traveled by wagon, train, steamboat, and horsedrawn cart. Masses of angry Indian men, anguished women, and children surrounded the little caravan as it left Fort Sill. Their shrill wails wrenched the hearts even of hardened soldiers.

During a brief stopover at Fort Leavenworth, Gray Beard attempted suicide. He cut a strip from his blanket and hanged himself from an iron bar in his window. His cellmates saved him, but the Cheyenne chief remained despondent. Later, on the train to Florida, he saw Pratt walking down the aisle with his six-year-old daughter. Gray Beard stopped Pratt and, speaking through an interpreter, said, "I have only one child, a daughter like yours. How would you like to have chains on your legs and be taken far from your home, your wife, and your child?"

"It was a hard question," Pratt later confessed.

Several Cheyenne urged Pratt to tie Gray Beard's hands, but he considered it unnecessary. He thought the chief seemed to cheer up as the days wore on—but he had a lot to learn. Despite leg irons, Gray Beard managed to jump through a window as the train slowed, approaching the Florida state line. Soldiers shouted an order to stop, but Gray Beard ignored it. He died from a gunshot through the chest.

Another suicide attempt marred the trip to Fort Marion. As the train approached Nashville, a Cheyenne named Lean Bear (a different Lean Bear from the one who met Lincoln) cut his throat with a penknife he had concealed. When two guards stepped in to help him, he stabbed them, too. Left for dead in Nashville, Lean Bear surprised everyone, including himself, by recovering. Forced to rejoin the prisoners at Fort Marion, including his own son, Lean Bear refused to talk or eat. He died of starvation at the prison.

FOLLOWING PAGES:
The Plains soon disappeared from view as the Indian prisoners traveled east. This short-grass prairie still stands in the High Plains of the Rita Blanca National Grassland near Dalhart, Texas.

Lurid local newspaper stories along the way trumpeted the pending arrival of the Indian prisoners. Typical is this comment from the *Leavenworth Daily Times,* May 9, 1875: "The hearts of our people were at last gladdened by a sight of the Indian captives, who arrived at Union Depot yesterday afternoon. The wild men . . . now held are charged with various crimes, arson, murder, rape, and robbery. The minor criminals are turned loose and are now roaming their respective reservations." Gawkers crowded the train stations as the prisoners passed through.

Leaving "Lean Bear" at Nashville

With the eye of a journalist, Zotom drew two dramatic moments on the journey. Above, the train idles in the Nashville railway station while uniformed men surround Lean Bear, who attempted suicide. Opposite, Gray Beard, despite shackles, leaps from a train window and hobbles down the tracks, only to be shot by guards.

Certainly the sight of so many white people unnerved the prisoners, and their anxiety was not helped by the taunts and insults shouted at them.

The Indians were prisoners of the Army, but the Bureau of Indian Affairs was responsible for their expenses. Neither department planned to spend money to make them comfortable or contribute to their welfare. Only Pratt, it appears, expected to see the prisoners rehabilitated, and he was determined to turn these young men into useful citizens. Nothing deterred him: not indifferent government bureaucrats, not cynical superiors, not insensitive townspeople who welcomed the increased tourism but did not want the Indians wandering city streets without an armed guard. In his prisoners, Pratt saw not criminals but talented young men simply following their traditional way of life. His vision made Fort Marion something other than a prison.

In fact, thanks to Pratt, Fort Marion became an Army camp, providing basic training to recruits. "It seemed best to get them out of the curio class," he later explained. "There was some objection by them to these changes, but by kindly persuasion it was gradually accomplished." Pratt did his best to improve living conditions for the prisoners, too. He

Killing of "Grey Beard" near Baldwin

had them build a large wooden barracks, which allowed them to move from humid, dank casement cells into lodgings with fresh air and ocean views. Wearing their uniforms with soldierly pride, the prisoners formed their own military company. They held their own military court and issued punishments for infractions, which violators readily accepted.

Pratt risked much in his openhanded treatment of the Indians. His superiors questioned the wisdom of his plan, but they let him run Fort Marion the way he chose. General Sherman, for one, predicted the Indians would one day cause him to regret his trust. Pratt promised to resign his commission if the Indians let him down—but they didn't. As he boasted in his memoirs, "a company of nearly fifty of the youngest men was organized and drilled, and for the remaining period of their three years imprisonment they guarded themselves without a material mishap."

Throughout the Indians' stay in Florida, Pratt peppered his military superiors with letters, notes, and reports. He kept them abreast of the progress they were making, assured Washington of their good behavior, and at the same time pleaded, cajoled, and demanded improvements in their care and status. To Gen. Philip Henry Sheridan, now Army

Originally put in dank casement cells, Pratt's Indian captives soon moved to large wooden barracks they helped construct on the terreplein atop the fort walls. From there, they could view the city of St. Augustine and Matanzas Bay.

commander of the Department of the Platte, from Iowa west to Idaho and Utah, he wrote: "These men are not hardened criminals. Most . . . have simply been following their leaders, much as a soldier obeys his officers, and [are] not really so culpable. Much can and should be done to reform these young men while under this banishment."

Pratt treated his Indian prisoners with dignity and respect and provided them with opportunities to mingle with the white community. He found work so the prisoners could earn money while in confinement. Clergymen conducted twice-weekly church services at the fort, and on Sundays prisoners could attend services in St. Augustine. But most important, Pratt opened the fort to women who taught the Indians how to read

and write. Within two years, Pratt reported that 47 of the younger men were receiving "good instruction" two hours a day, five days a week, and that upwards of 30 of them could read and understand the first-level reader. "They are just in that state of advancement," he boasted, "where they can understand and make themselves understood, and their progress increases every day."

Pratt's program proved so successful that even the most diehard military cynics grudgingly conceded that he had rehabilitated seemingly incorrigible criminals. The Indians were so pleased with their new way of life that they repeatedly asked to have their families join them and to be sent somewhere more appropriate to learn the white man's ways.

Government officials turned a deaf ear on Pratt's recommendations and responded equally hardheartedly to Indian appeals. One request came, for example, from the Kiowa chief Mamanti, forwarded by Pratt to superiors in June 1875: "Tell 'Washington' to give us our women and children and send us to a country where we can work and live like white men.

"There are a great many Indians at Fort Sill and in that country who have done more bad work than we have," Mamanti argued, asking "why should they be allowed to go free, and be happy with their families and we are sent down here as prisoners to live in these dark cells? That is not right."

Claiming to have heard similar statements a hundred times, General Sheridan dismissed Mamanti's eloquent plea as mere "Indian

THE FORT MARION EXPERIENCE

twaddle." All the Indians at St. Augustine, Sheridan reminded Pratt, were unmitigated murderers who acted without provocation. To keep from being pestered by more such petitions, though, Sheridan approved the general request—but only for each man's immediate family circle.

That request got no further than the Commissioner of Indian Affairs, whose budget would have been tapped for transporting and supporting the dependents. Dismissing Pratt as inexperienced and endorsing Sheridan's notion that such speech was twaddle, the commissioner squelched any notion of family reunions. He claimed the move would involve 300 people and would cause more harm than good: The women would doubtless become prostitutes and their children would have to be taken out of school!

If there was any twaddle in this situation, it came from the commissioner. The actual count of dependents was 90. Although one unmarried Kiowa asked his family to send him a wife, she would have been offset by the Cheyenne with two wives who asked to be sent only one—the one who most wanted to live in Florida! With regard to education, their children would have been far better off in St. Augustine than at home, where efforts at Indian education had barely begun. Mamanti died a month after making his plea.

Fort Marion—now called by its original Spanish name, Castillo de San Marcos—is the oldest European fort in the United States. Once the government's prison of choice for Indians considered troublesome, today it is a national monument.

*T*he callousness of Washington, whoever "Washington" might be, bitterly disappointed both the prisoners and Pratt. He ingratiatingly admitted that the prisoners had been "unmitigated murderers of men, women, and children." But they had been the worst of their people because they were the most active, he argued, and they would become the best of their people for the same reason—"if permitted and aided to it." Therefore, he advised, "it is protection to ourselves to open wide the door of civilization, and even drive them to it while we can, if we find that necessary. But we will not find it necessary—they will enter of themselves. They may flag, but under proper management, will recover and push ahead."

As part of his civilization program, Pratt encouraged the Indians to draw, and he supplied them with paper, pencils, and inks. The result was a prodigious outpouring of artistic expression. During their three years in prison, the Indians in Fort Marion rendered hundreds of drawings and filled scores of tablets that they sold to tourists and visitors and that today are treasured by museums, galleries, and collectors. They also carved bows and arrows, polished seashells, and made paper cutouts, all for sale.

Pratt documented changes in the Indians he cared for by having one photograph taken as they arrived in their tribal garb and another after they had received haircuts and uniforms.

After visiting the fort in 1877, Harriet Beecher Stowe, author of *Uncle Tom's Cabin,* wrote a long article for *Harper's Weekly* in which she marveled at the products the prisoners made. "All along I saw traces of Indian skill and ingenuity in the distinctive work of the tribes," she wrote. "Bows and arrows skillfully made and painted, sea shells nicely polished, paper toys representing horses, warriors and buffaloes, showing a good deal of rude artistic skill and spirit in the design and coloring, were disposed here and there to attract the eye and tempt the purse of the visitors." Pratt told Stowe that the Indians had thus far grossed more than $5,000. The income was theirs to keep, and most sent the money home to their families.

Henry Benjamin Whipple, an Episcopal bishop from Minnesota, lived in St. Augustine one winter for health reasons and became a frequent visitor to Fort Marion. He patronized its graphic arts program, buying numerous drawing books and presenting them to influential individuals as proof of the progress Pratt was making with the prisoners.

"I was never more touched than when I entered this school," Whipple informed President Ulysses S. Grant. "Here were men who had committed murder upon helpless women and children sitting like docile children at the feet of the women, learning to read."

Several prisoners used drawings as pictograph letters to communicate with loved ones at home. Pictograph letters also enabled the prisoners to learn of the great Indian victory at the Little Bighorn in June 1876, midway through their imprisonment. The news arrived in the form of a large pictograph from the Northern Cheyenne, detailing their part in Custer's destruction. Drawn on the back of a blank muster roll, probably part of the plunder from the fight, the drawing showed the various bands fleeing from pursuit after the battle, with Sitting Bull heading for Canada. "It was of such historical interest," Pratt declared, "that I sent it to General Sheridan, who acknowledged its receipt and value." Sadly, this unique document has since been lost.

*A*fter three years at Fort Marion, Pratt finally prevailed on the government to free the prisoners. Twenty-two of the young men chose to remain in the East. Of these, five went to New England for religious studies; the rest, accompanied by Pratt, went to Hampton College in Virginia, a school for freedmen established after the Civil War. Once they were enrolled there, Pratt questioned the decision. He was fearful that prejudice against blacks would be transferred to the Indians if they stayed at Hampton, and he soon persuaded the Army to establish a separate school for Indians at Carlisle Barracks in Pennsylvania.

Pratt welcomed visitors to Fort Marion, such as these unidentified men and women. Author and abolitionist Harriet Beecher Stowe visited a class there and marveled at the "dark men in the United States uniform, neat, compact, trim, with well-brushed boots and nicely kept clothing and books in their hands."

Pratt had advocated that family members be brought to Fort Marion, predicting that if they were not, the prisoners' return home could be disastrous. Family members back West had not experienced the changes the Florida internment had generated. To a great extent his prediction proved to be painfully accurate for the 40-some survivors who did return to the West. The Army escorted them to their reservations, then simply turned them loose with no direction, no assistance, and no opportunity to use their education or training.

Left on their own, the former prisoners merged into the general Indian population. When asked if the returned Kiowa and Comanche seemed to have profited from the education and civilizing efforts at St. Augustine, the commanding officer at Fort Sill replied, "I do not think the extent [of influence] amounts to much. . . . The St. Augustine Indians can write a few words, sing a hymn or two, but are wanting in a knowledge of the industrial pursuits of life. The consequence is they find the larger number of their tribal associates far better off than they are, and it would not be strange if they lapsed into their former savage ways of life. These opinions," he wrote, "are concurred in by . . . the Post interpreter, and many of the best Indians on the reservation."

His candidly harsh assessment is not surprising. Even today, Indians who leave their reservations for college or employment have a difficult readjustment, if and when they do return. Imagine what it must have been like for the Fort Marion prisoners a century ago.

Never again did the tribes of the Southern Plains offer armed resistance to the white man's road. This time the clear victor was the U.S. Army. The Army strategy of convergence and harassment had given the militants no rest and had brought hostilities to a quick and relatively bloodless conclusion.

If it had worked so well on the Southern Plains, some now argued, why not on the Northern Plains, toward which the eyes of the nation now turned? ⤶

PRATT'S VISION

✳

*H*aving defeated the tribes of the Plains militarily, the United States government undertook a massive campaign to transform the Indians culturally and economically. The goals were to eradicate "Indian-ness" and to assimilate Indians into white society. The best way to accomplish this, officials believed, was to educate Indian children.

The flagship of the government boarding schools was the Carlisle Indian Industrial School, established in Army barracks in southern Pennsylvania by Capt. Richard H. Pratt. After managing the Indian prison at Fort Marion, Pratt became committed to improving the lives and futures of Indian children. Ten thousand children enrolled in his school during its 40-year existence. The school flourished from 1879 to 1918, by which time it and similar schools were falling out of favor.

At these schools, the young Indians learned skilled trades, farming, and home economics, but they received little more than an eighth-grade education. When they graduated, they faced tremendous difficulties. Successfully educated out of their traditional cultural patterns, they still did not easily fit into the white culture that had transformed them, and hence they did not comfortably belong to either culture.

At the time, though, it was impossible to predict such a difficult future for the children of the Carlisle School. Even Indians praised the work that Pratt was doing. Geronimo visited the school in 1905 and told the children he met there, "You are here to study, to learn the ways of white men, do it well."

Pratt's experience as a cavalry officer in the Southern Plains and then as the commanding officer of the Florida Indian prison gave him insight into Indian personalities and customs, which informed his work at the Carlisle School.

In 1879 Pratt founded the Carlisle Indian Industrial School in Pennsylvania, where

thousands of Indian girls and boys learned farming, home economics, and skilled trades.

*"I called to my men,
'This is a good day to die. Follow me!'
Every man whipped another man's horse
and we rushed right upon them."*

— LOW DOG, AN OGLALA CHIEF AT THE
BATTLE OF THE LITTLE BIGHORN

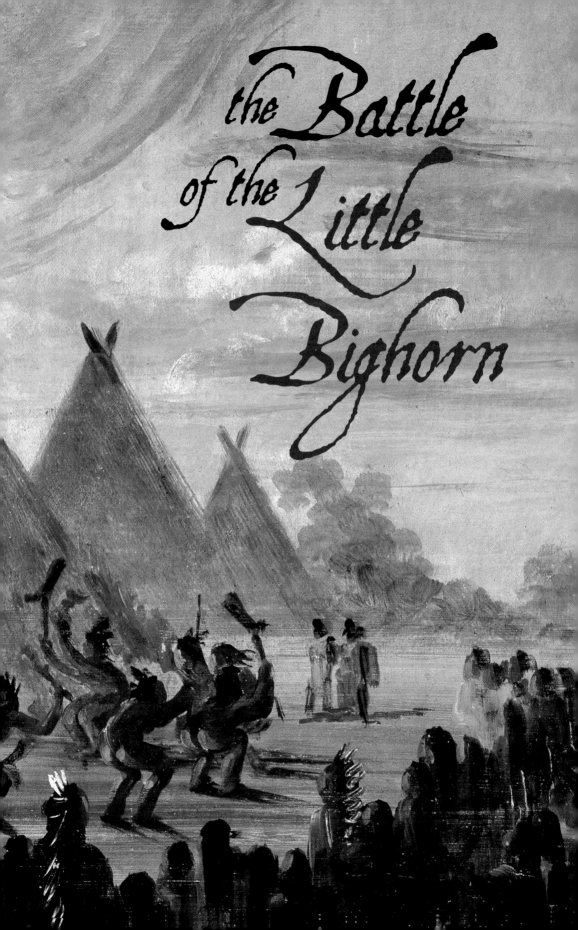

the Battle of the Little Bighorn

In 1874 Gen. George A. Custer invited reporters and miners to accompany his train of one hundred or more wagons into Dakota Territory. The discovery of gold set off a mining stampede, violating the Fort Laramie Treaty and precipitating the Battle at the Little Bighorn.

1876

✳

The wagons carrying the prisoners to Florida were scarcely out of sight of Fort Sill before the Western Army turned its attention, in 1875, to the Northern Plains. Despite the vast expanse of the Great Sioux Reservation, essentially the size of present-day South Dakota, it was still too confining for the free-roaming bands. No one knew how many bands of Indians were still resisting reservation life; they fluctuated with the weather and the hunting. The Army's task was to force these bands onto the reservation. Conflict seemed inevitable.

The resisting Indians included members of several tribes, primarily Sioux but also Northern Arapaho and Cheyenne. Their leader was Sitting Bull, a Hunkpapa medicine man and proven warrior. Crafty and charismatic, astute and intelligent, he had utter disdain for the white man's road and those who bought into it. "I am a red man," Sitting Bull proclaimed. "If the Great Spirit had desired me to be a white man, he would have made me so in the first place. It is not necessary for eagles to be crows. Now we are poor, but we are free. . . . I do not wish to be shut up in a corral. . . . All reservation Indians I have seen are worthless. They are neither red warriors nor white farmers. They are neither wolf nor dog."

Sitting Bull had not signed the Treaty of Fort Laramie, nor had his able lieutenants: Gall, a Hunkpapa chief, and his adopted brother; Hump, a Miniconjou chief; Lame White Man, a Cheyenne chief; and the mystical Crazy Horse. Since his debut at Red Cloud's ambush of Fetterman a decade earlier, Crazy Horse had emerged as an incomparable war leader, bold in battle and seemingly protected by an aura that bullets could not penetrate.

Indians roaming the large, open areas of the Northern Plains did not represent an immediate danger to white men and women—unlike their Southern Plains kinsmen, who viewed the people of Texas as another form of game to hunt. The mere presence of Indians, still free on the Plains, rattled many settlers, though. Government officials were doing all they could to convince the "treaty Indians"—those abiding by government rules—that the white road was the best, and free-roaming bands

PRECEDING PAGES: George Catlin painted "War Dance, Sioux" in Europe in the 1840s, but he based it on sketches he made at Fort Pierre in 1832.

hindered that process. Granted, some Northern Plains Indians took the scalp of an unwary traveler or two, and some hunted outside the boundaries of the Great Sioux Reservation, but all these reasons added up did not justify the government decision to classify them as hostiles.

When the government authorized the construction of the Northern Pacific Railroad through the Dakota and Montana Territories, the heart of Lakota country, conflicts between settlers and non-treaty Indians were bound to come to a head. Aware of the danger, the Army decided it needed to build a new fort to guard the railroad. It would be located in the southwestern portion of the Great Sioux Reservation, in the Black Hills, a region long sacred to the tribes of the Northern Plains. It was in the Black Hills that the Cheyenne prophet Sweet Medicine received the four sacred arrows from the Creator, and it was to the Black Hills that young men went on vision quests, solo spiritual coming-of-age journeys. Many still do.

Mathew Brady photographed this portrait of George Armstrong Custer, his wife, Libbie, and his brother, Tom, who would die with him at the Little Bighorn. The three were almost inseparable.

The officer leading the Black Hills expedition was George Armstrong Custer, transferred to the Dakotas one year before. The boy general of the Civil War chafed at his present rank of lieutenant colonel and hungered for the limelight. He led his troops out from Fort Abraham Lincoln "to see what he could find." He evidently had more in mind than finding a site for the fort, though, because his entourage included newspaper reporters and miners. When those miners discovered gold, it set off a stampede. News of the gold strike reached Fort Abraham Lincoln before Custer's column had even returned. Soon hundreds of prospectors were tramping through the Black Hills, caring nothing about reservation boundaries or the spiritual significance of the region.

With the country overrun with prospectors and the Army unable to keep them off Lakota land, the government attempted to buy the Black Hills. Lakota leaders scoffed at the idea. Outraged and frustrated, U.S. officials recommended military action against Sitting Bull and his allies, charging that they were failing to meet the terms of the 1868 Treaty of Fort Laramie—a trumped-up charge at best, since most of the Indians involved had not been party to the treaty and were living on unceded lands. Regardless, the government sent messengers to the free-roaming bands, telling them, "Come to the reservation or be considered hostiles against whom the United States Army will make war."

On the deadline set for them, January 31, 1876, the Indians did not appear. The Army went into action. Between March and May, three

columns of soldiers traveled to Montana, led by Gen. George Crook, Col. John Gibbon, and Gen. Alfred Terry, whose orders were to find the Indians and force them onto the reservation. At the same time, the Indian camps were swelling. After Crook attacked a Cheyenne village on the Powder River, the Lakota and Cheyenne bands began camping together for mutual protection. Young men leaving the reservation were joining these camps as well. They admired Sitting Bull and wanted to join him in his effort to drive white people from the Black Hills.

The Indians were not anxious to fight a full-scale war, but neither were they afraid of the soldiers. They were well armed: In fact, some carried better rifles than those issued to Army soldiers, thanks to traders who provided them the finest in modern weaponry. One more event gave them added confidence. While the village camped near Medicine Deer Rock, near today's town of Lame Deer, Sitting Bull received a vision.

It had come to him as part of a sacred Sun Dance, performed for spiritual guidance. Sitting Bull had promised the Great Spirit that he

Officers and wives of the Seventh Cavalry enjoy a leisurely moment in front of General Custer's quarters at Fort Abraham Lincoln in 1875.

FOLLOWING PAGES:
Indians past and present regard the Badlands of South Dakota, west of the Black Hills, as sacred ground.

would cut one hundred pieces of flesh from his body as an expression of self-sacrifice. "I fulfilled my vow," Sitting Bull declared. "My brother Jumping Bull cut tiny pieces of skin—fifty from each arm—using an awl and a sharp knife. I danced two days and two nights. God sent me a vision. I saw white soldiers and enemy Indians on horseback falling into the Sioux camp. They were coming down like grasshoppers, headfirst, with their hats falling off. Just then I heard a voice from above, saying, 'I give you these because they have no ears.'" To Sitting Bull, this detail referred to the Army's failure to heed the warnings of the Sioux to keep off their land.

On June 17, scouts brought word back to the Indian camp that Army soldiers were marching in their direction along nearby Rosebud Creek. Crazy Horse led a large force of Lakota and Cheyenne out to meet General Crook and his troops. Their encounter, named the Battle of the Rosebud, lasted six hours and ended only after the Indians tired of fighting. The Indians left, and the soldiers retreated. What saved Crook's infantry from disaster was the vigilance and bravery of his Indian auxiliaries—some 200 Shoshone and Crow scouts, whose skilled horsemanship kept the Lakota and Cheyenne attack at bay while the white soldiers assumed battle formation.

Meanwhile Gibbon and Terry, unaware of Crook's defeat, met at the mouth of the Rosebud on the Yellowstone River. Terry sent Custer and the Seventh Cavalry, some 600 strong, to follow a fresh Indian trail leading to the Bighorn River, a favorite hunting area and campground of the Northern tribes. Custer's orders were just to locate the village. The infantry with Gibbon and Terry were then to follow as quickly as possible. The plan was that the troops would unite and attack the village from at least two sides.

Indian scouts, 40 Arikara and 6 Crow, traveled with Custer. Indians served the U.S. military as scouts for most campaigns, from the American Revolution until the end of the Indian wars. Although some may view them as traitors for helping the Army fight the Indian, this attitude overlooks intertribal warfare that long predated the arrival of the white man. As late as the 1860s and 1870s, the Crow and Arikara still suffered from Lakota and Cheyenne aggression. Understandably, then, they viewed the Army as allies in their centuries-old struggle for survival against a determined and more numerous enemy—but, unfortunately, failed to realize that in helping the United States defeat their enemies, they were dooming themselves to life on a reservation.

The Crow—who called Custer "Son of the Morning Star"—were especially anxious to even old scores. For generations, surrounded by tribal

Gen. George Crook finished near the bottom of his West Point class but went on to a stellar career in the Civil War and the Far West. Later in life, Crook sought better treatment for the Indians against whom he had campaigned.

OPPOSITE: *In 1876, Sitting Bull's influence extended across the Northern Plains. No other Lakota chief approached his political and spiritual power.*

enemies and greatly outnumbered, the Crow had had to stand alone. Constant warfare made them hardy, brave, and cunning. That is why six of their young men were riding with Custer and the Seventh Cavalry on June 25, 1876.

One of those Crow scouts was White Man Runs Him, great uncle (considered grandfather by Indian custom) to Dr. Joseph Medicine Crow, the official historian of the Crow Indians today. Dr. Medicine Crow, now in his 90s, personally knew five of Custer's six Crow scouts. As a youngster, he was the interpreter when historians came to interview White Man Runs Him about the events at the Little Bighorn. According to him, the Crows warned Custer that Sitting Bull's village was too large for the Seventh to attack on its own. They urged him to wait for reinforcements, but this he refused to do. He thought the Lakota in the village had spotted him and would escape, thereby depriving him of the victory he so desperately wanted.

The scouts recognized that Custer did not plan to take their advice. Convinced they would all die, they dismounted at one of the rest stops. They removed their Army clothing and transformed themselves into traditional Crow warriors, putting on their war clothes, including buckskin leggings and face paint, in preparation for possible death. Dr. Medicine Crow collected this story from the scouts.

"What are they doing?" Custer asked Mitch Bouyer, his interpreter, who was half white and half Sioux and could speak the Crow language.

Once Bouyer translated, one of the scouts pointed his finger at Custer: "Tell him that in a very short time we are all going to be killed. I intend to go to 'the other side of the camp' dressed as a Crow warrior, not a white man."

This defeatist attitude angered Custer, who said something like: "Tell those superstitious Indians to get the hell out of here. If they are so afraid of the Lakota, we'll do the fighting, and they can go home." Bouyer, however, told the scouts, "You are fortunate. He says you can go now. You have completed your work. You have found the Sioux. Go now! Hurry! Don't stop!"

Although released, the scouts did not leave immediately. White Swan and Half Yellow Face joined one of Custer's units, led by Maj. Marcus Reno, and one of them, White Swan, got severely injured. Another, named Curley, joined some Arikara who made off with a goodly number of Sioux horses. The other three—White Man Runs Him, Goes Ahead, and Hairy Moccasin—joined the same unit for a time but then slipped away.

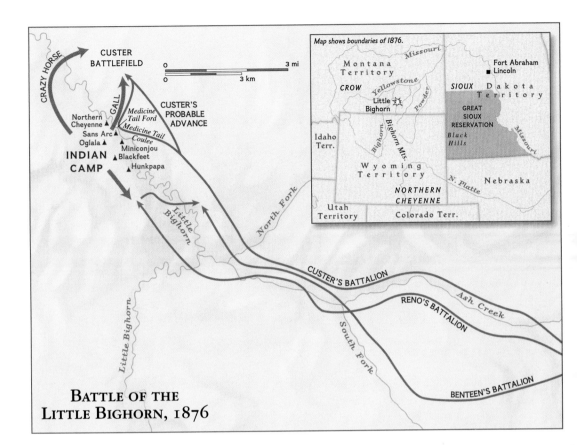

Map shows boundaries of 1876.

0 ——— 3 mi
0 ——— 3 km

CUSTER
BATTLEFIELD

CRAZY HORSE

GALL

CUSTER'S
PROBABLE
ADVANCE

Northern
Cheyenne ▲
Sans Arc ▲
Oglala ▲
Minconjou
Blackfeet
▲ Hunkpapa

INDIAN
CAMP

Medicine
Tail Ford
Medicine Tail
Coulee

Little
Bighorn

North Fork

Little Bighorn

South Fork

CUSTER'S BATTALION

RENO'S BATTALION

Ash Creek

BENTEEN'S BATTALION

Montana
Territory

Missouri

Yellowstone

CROW

Little
Bighorn

Powder

Bighorn Mts.

Idaho
Terr.

Wyoming
Territory

NORTHERN
CHEYENNE

Utah
Territory

Colorado Terr.

Fort Abraham
■ Lincoln

SIOUX Dakota
Territory

GREAT
SIOUX
RESERVATION

Black
Hills

Missouri

N. Platte

Nebraska

**BATTLE OF THE
LITTLE BIGHORN, 1876**

As a result, none of the Crow scouts shared the fate of Son of the Morning Star and the cavalry troops who died with him.

The Crow scouts had not exaggerated. The village was certainly the largest they had ever seen. Some 1,200 tepees and brush wickiups stood in six large tribal circles. One circle belonged to the Northern Cheyenne, the other five to the Lakota—Hunkpapa, Oglala, Miniconjou, Sans Arc, and Blackfeet. The village stretched for about three miles along the Little Bighorn River, called the Greasy Grass by the Indians. In it were upwards of 10,000 people, including as many as 1,500 fighting men. The horse herd was gigantic, estimated at 25,000. "It was a very big village and you could hardly count the tepees," recalled Black Elk, the Oglala holy man, who was then 13 years old. "Along the side towards the east was the Greasy Grass, with some timber along it, and it was running full from the melting of the snow in the Bighorn Mountains. . . . On the westward side of us were lower hills, and there we grazed our ponies and guarded them. There were so many they could not be counted."

FOLLOWING PAGES:
Gentle grassy mounds punctuate the terrain around the Little Bighorn River today, belying the violent battle fought there more than a century ago.

Sitting Bull

tatankaiyotake
oki'ci'ze itočou

took part in a sacred pipe ceremony to seal the peace, in the lodge of the keeper of the sacred arrows of the Cheyenne people. Speaking in Cheyenne, the arrow keeper warned Custer of disaster if he ever betrayed the pact of friendship he had just made with the Cheyenne people. The holy man then ended the ceremony in dramatic fashion by tapping the pipe bowl on the toe of Custer's boot and spilling the ashes on the ground.

By attacking them at the Little Bighorn, the Cheyenne believe, Custer broke the pact and angered the spirits that protected the tribe. This interpretation, known to young and old alike, is central to Cheyenne oral history versions of the Battle of the Little Bighorn.

A second story, less widely told, claims that Custer captured a Cheyenne woman at the Battle of the Washita and later fathered a son by her. The opportunity certainly was there, because the Seventh Cavalry did return to Fort Hays with a number of Cheyenne women and children. Capt. Miles Keogh evidently enjoyed the spoils of war, as he wrote in a letter from Fort Hays: "We have here about ninety squaws— from our last fight [at the Washita]—some of them are very pretty. I have one that is quite intelligent. It is usual for officers to have two or three lounging around."

Captain Benteen, no fan of Custer's, later charged him with keeping a Cheyenne woman named Monahsetah as his mistress, a woman whom Custer himself singles out for her rare beauty in his book, *My Life on the Plains*. The daughter of Chief Little Rock, she was seven months pregnant when captured and did remain with the Seventh Cavalry for several months, serving as an intermediary with her people.

In 1927, Thomas Marquis interviewed Kate Big Head, a Northern Cheyenne woman who witnessed the Battle of the Little Bighorn. She remembered Custer's visit to the Cheyenne. "We were far westward, on a branch of the river the whites call Red River, I think. This time there was no fighting. Custer smoked the peace pipe with the Cheyenne chiefs. He promised never again to fight the Cheyenne, so all of us Cheyennes followed him to the soldier fort—Fort Sill. Our people gave him the name Mi-es-tzie, meaning Long Hair."

The Cheyenne women considered Custer handsome, Kate Big Head recalled, but her cousin Me-o-tzi [Monahsetah] had his eye. "She often went with him to help find the trails of the Indians. . . . All of the Cheyennes liked her, and they were glad she had a place so important in life. After Long Hair went away, different ones of the Cheyenne young men wanted to marry her, but she would not have any of them. She said

Red Horse (above), a Miniconjou Lakota chief, participated in the Battle of the Little Bighorn and later drew a series of 41 pictographs about it, using colored pencils and ink on brown manila paper. The split drawing (opposite) shows the hoof tracks of Reno's troopers approaching Sitting Bull's village and, on the right, triumphant warriors forcing a retreat.

that Long Hair was her husband and had promised to come back to her. . . . She waited for seven years and then he was killed."

After the battle, according to Kate Big Head, two Southern Cheyenne women came across Custer's body. "While they were there looking at him some Sioux men came up and were about to cut up the body. The Cheyenne women, thinking of Me-o-tzi, signed to them, 'He is a relative of ours.' The men cut off his little finger but otherwise did not mutilate the body. The women then pushed the point of an awl through his ears. This was done, they said, to improve his hearing in the afterlife, as it seemed he had not heard what our chiefs had said when he smoked the pipe of peace with them."

Several Cheyenne at the Lame Deer reservation tell a similar story, which might be dismissed but for the condition of Custer's body: relatively unmarked except for bullet wounds to the chest and the side of the head and an arrow shoved up his penis. Those who examined his body found blood that had come from his ears but speculated the cause to be either the obvious gunshot to the head or a less obvious bullet that had entered and exited his ears. Perhaps—but the arrow shoved up his penis (rarely mentioned out of concern for his widow, Libbie Custer) and the blood from his ears could also have been the work of angry Cheyenne women, remembering a jilted lover and unkept promises to their people.

White Man Runs Him, photographed by Delancy Gill in 1910, was a teenager when he and five other Crow Indians served as U.S. Army scouts assisting the Seventh Cavalry at the Battle of the Little Bighorn. Of his Crow scouts, Custer wrote, "They are magnificent-looking men, so much handsomer and more Indian-like than any we have ever seen, and so jolly and sportive; nothing of the gloomy, silent redman about them."

Despite their defeat, Custer's troops received high praise for valor from many of their Indian combatants. "I tell no lies about dead men," said Sitting Bull. "These men who came with Long Hair were as good men as ever fought."

His opinion was endorsed by Low Dog, an Oglala chief. "I never before nor since saw men so brave and fearless as those white warriors," Low Dog declared. "I called to my men, 'This is a good day to die. Follow me!' We massed our men, and that no man should fall back, every man whipped another man's horse and we rushed right upon them."

The Lakota and Cheyenne could have pressed their attack on the soldiers huddled with Reno and Benteen on the bluffs across the river. The morning after Custer's destruction, hundreds of warriors, many armed with captured rifles and pistols, kept up a terrific fire on the trapped soldiers, but Sitting Bull stopped the attack. "Let them go," he declared. "Let them live. They have come against us, and we have killed a few. If we kill them all, they will send a bigger army against us."

Sitting Bull had indeed won a great victory. Altogether, the Indians killed 263 men, including 3 Arikara scouts: 212 with Custer and 51 with Reno. Indian fatalities were far fewer: Perhaps as few as 30 or so warriors were killed, although a number of the wounded died later. Some of the Indians who died were suicide warriors who had vowed beforehand to be killed in battle. A few Indians were accidentally killed or wounded in the crossfire because the thick dust and smoke sometimes made it impossible to tell friend from foe. Several women and children died in the initial attack on the village.

When the Indians in the huge village on the Little Bighorn heard that another group of soldiers was rapidly approaching, they set to moving camp almost immediately. By noon the next day, Sitting Bull and his followers were wending their way across the open prairie toward the Bighorn Mountains, seeking a place of safety where the wounded could rest and all could celebrate their victory. In their wake, they left a blazing prairie fire. If the Army chose to follow them, they wanted to be sure that their horses could find no forage along the way. ⤺

CUSTER'S SCOUTS

✳

The story of the Battle of the Little Bighorn has been told and retold in countless books and movies, but the fact that nearly 50 Crow and Arikara warriors rode at Custer's side that day is all but lost in the fascination.

The Arikara were assigned not to fight but to scout ahead of the troops during the long campaign. They were to supply the officers with fresh meat and to carry messages back to Fort Abraham Lincoln. Despite their willingness to help the Army and the valuable service they provided during the campaign and in the final fight, the Arikara have become the forgotten warriors of the Battle of the Little Bighorn. This oversight remains a source of discontent to the descendants of the scouts, who still live on the Fort Berthold Reservation in North Dakota.

In truth, the Battle of the Little Bighorn was as much an intertribal conflict among Indians as it was a battle between Indians and white men. Custer's tribal allies are largely forgotten today, despite the facts that three of them, all Arikara, were killed and that two, one Arikara and one Crow, were wounded.

After the battle, the Crow and Arikara people suffered confinement to reservations. They shared the fate faced by the tribes they had fought against, and thus felt betrayed by the government they had sought to help.

Photographed during the 1874 Black Hills Expedition, George Armstrong Custer assumed the romantic posture he cherished, hunting hound at his feet and scouts surrounding him, including Arikara Bloody Knife, pointing, and Goose, standing in the doorway.

Goose, shot in the hand at Little Bighorn, was one of the Arikara Indians who agreed to help the Seventh Cavalry in the 1876 campaign.

Mitch Bouyer (above), half Lakota, half French, served as interpreter for the Crow scouts with the Seventh Cavalry. Bouyer told the scouts to leave, but he stayed and died with Custer. Also killed that day was Little Brave (below), an Arikara scout.

Four of the six Crow scouts who fought at the Little Bighorn—left to right, White Man Runs Him, Hairy Moccasin, Curley, and Goes Ahead—stand among tombstones on the battlefield in 1908. Continually pestered to pose and tell their battle stories, even they could shed little light on what actually happened on that fateful day in 1876.

"Hear me my chiefs! I am tired.
My heart is sick and sad.
From where the sun now stands,
I will fight no more forever."

— CHIEF JOSEPH, SURRENDERING
ON BEHALF OF THE NEZ PERCE

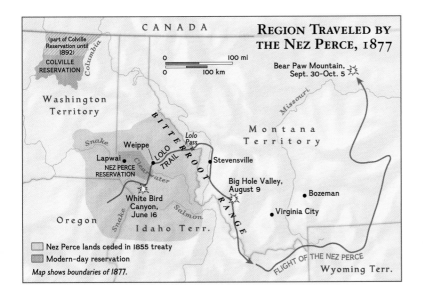

REGION TRAVELED BY
THE NEZ PERCE, 1877

CANADA

(part of Colville
Reservation until
1892)
COLVILLE
RESERVATION

Washington
Territory

Bear Paw Mountain,
Sept. 30–Oct. 5

100 mi

100 km

Montana
Territory

Missouri

Columbia

Snake

BITTERROOT RANGE

Lolo
Pass

LOLO TRAIL

Weippe

Lapwai
NEZ PERCE
RESERVATION

Clearwater

Stevensville

Big Hole Valley,
August 9

Bozeman

White Bird
Canyon,
June 16

Virginia City

Oregon

Salmon

Snake

Idaho Terr.

Nez Perce lands ceded in 1855 treaty
Modern-day reservation
Map shows boundaries of 1877.

FLIGHT OF THE NEZ PERCE
Wyoming Terr.

Lewis and Clark spent several weeks with the Nez Perce and admired their beautiful women, as evidenced by the children fathered during their stay. Tzi-kal-tza, opposite, said to be the son of William Clark, joined Chief Joseph in flight from Idaho when he was 72.

difficult under the best of circumstances, but the Army made it more so by ordering the free-roaming bands onto the reservation in one month, threatening dire consequences if they missed the June 15 deadline. Joseph pleaded for more time. To get to the reservation, the Indians had to cross the Snake River, swollen with spring meltwaters. Moreover, the Indians had thousands of cattle and horses; many were foaling and calving. No matter, responded the Army officials. The Indians had to obey. The crossing was made without loss of life, but hundreds of animals drowned or were left behind, only to be snapped up by white neighbors.

Once they had crossed the Snake, the bands decided to rest and enjoy their freedom for a few more days before moving onto the reservation. While they camped there, a young man named Wahlitis, whose father had been murdered by a white settler the year before, got drunk with two friends and began challenging the decision to go so meekly onto the reservation.

An old man mocked them. "Why don't you kill the white man who killed your father?" he challenged. Now publicly ridiculed, the three young men rode off to a nearby settlement on the Salmon River, seeking the man who had killed Wahlitis's father. They failed to find him, but they killed four white men, wounded another, then rode back to camp and displayed the guns and horses taken from their victims. Seeing the trophies, another angry young warrior named Big Dawn jumped onto one of the captured horses and galloped through the village, yelling, "Now you will have to go to war! Wahlitis has killed white men and stolen their horses. Now the soldiers will be coming after us. Prepare for war!"

*FOLLOWING PAGES:
On their way from Idaho to Montana, the Nez Perce traveled through mountain vistas such as Blodgett Canyon, east of the Bitterroots.*

1877

141

Joseph had been away during the murders, but he felt responsible, even though the boys who had committed them belonged to Chief White Bird's band. "I was deeply grieved," Joseph later said. "I know that my young men did a great wrong, but I ask, 'Who was first to blame?' They had been insulted a thousand times. Their fathers and brothers had been killed. Their mothers and wives had been disgraced. They had been driven to madness by the whiskey sold to them by the white men.

"I deny that either my father or myself ever sold that land," Joseph continued. "It may never again be our home, but my father sleeps there. And I love it as I love my mother. I left there hoping to avoid bloodshed, but I knew that I must lead my people in the fight, for the white people would not believe my story."

The news of the murders shocked the other Indians in the camp. Some rushed to the Lapwai reservation to avoid further trouble. Others fled south to the canyon of White Bird Creek, a deep, remote, spectacular gorge. Joseph waited two days while his wife gave birth to a daughter, then joined the others at White Bird Canyon.

The ranking Army officer on the scene was Gen. O. O. Howard, the one-armed general of Civil War fame who now commanded all the troops in the Northwest. It was Howard who had ordered the Nez Perce to report within one month, prompting the anger that led to hostilities. When he recognized that the Indians were ignoring his orders, he sent Capt. David Perry and two companies of the First Cavalry to round them up. Several volunteers joined Perry, giving him a force of 110. The Indian camp in White Bird Canyon included no more than 60 fighting men, many too young or too old to be considered warriors. A third were armed with bows and arrows; the rest had mediocre guns, antiquated muzzle loaders. None of the Nez Perce were battle-tested. Perry expected to make quick work of them.

When the Nez Perce saw Perry's force approaching at dawn, June 16, they sent several men under a flag of truce to meet them. Ignoring the white flag, the soldiers opened fire, then charged. Instead of retreating, the Indians fought back, completely routing the inexperienced Army troops. One group of 19 soldiers died to a man, trapped against a rocky wall. The Nez Perce killed 34 and wounded 4, suffering only 2 or 3 wounded themselves. More important, they collected some threescore rifles and pistols and considerable ammunition. Other than that, they left the bodies alone. There was no scalping, no mutilation of the dead.

General Howard summoned reinforcements from across the Pacific Northwest. Meanwhile the Nez Perce belligerents, thanks to Army stupidity, increased in number. Based on rumors that he was going to join the hostiles, two cavalry troops attacked the village of Chief Looking Glass, camping peaceably on the reservation near Lapwai. Everyone in the village fled, abandoning tents, horses, and belongings. A stray bullet killed an Indian baby. The unwarranted attack so infuriated the villagers that they left the reservation and joined the hostile force, which now totaled about 200 men and 600 women and children.

For several days, the Nez Perce traveled through the twisted landscape along the Clearwater River, uncertain what to do. As they camped on a plateau, General Howard and 400 troops caught them completely by surprise, opening fire with a howitzer and two Gatling guns from a bluff across the river. Again, instead of fleeing, the Indians counterattacked. Led by Toohoolhoolzote, an elderly but able leader, two dozen warriors dashed across the Clearwater, scrambled up the bluffs, and held the soldiers at bay. Howard, to his great embarrassment, found himself besieged for more than a day, even though he had artillery and a force that outnumbered the enemy six to one. When Army reinforcements arrived, though, the Indian attackers became the attacked. By the time the shooting stopped, the Nez Perce camp had made its escape at the cost of only 4 killed and 6 wounded. Howard's losses were 13 killed and 23 wounded.

The fugitives headed east until they reached Weippe Prairie, a favored camas campground where their people had first met Lewis and Clark. Until this point, the Nez Perce had been five separate bands, thrown together by circumstances and simply trying to defend themselves. Now the time had come to make some decisions. The leaders—Joseph, his younger brother Ollokot, Toohoolhoolzote, White Bird, Looking Glass, and others—held a council. No one had a clear plan. Joseph wanted to stay and defend his homeland. Looking Glass, whose band had frequently hunted buffalo on the Montana plains to the east, thought otherwise. They must leave Idaho, he advised. Farther east, they would be safe. They could either join the Crow in Montana or the Lakota in Canada. After a few years, once these troubles had been forgotten, Looking Glass believed, they could return home.

The leaders agreed to this desperate plan to leave their troubles behind them. Looking Glass was appointed war chief for the united band, which set out on its epic trek over the heavily forested Lolo Trail: 800 people, some sick, some wounded, men, women, children, driving 2,000

Chief Joseph had four wives and with them many children. This portrait, taken in 1878 or 1879, includes three wives and two children. It was taken in Kansas when Joseph was about 40 years old, in exile from his homeland.

horses. Pressing them from behind was General Howard, who needed 40 woodchoppers to hack a road so his Army could follow the Indian trail.

Once in Montana, the fugitives felt safe. They bought supplies in Stevensville, then moved onto a campground in the Big Hole Valley to rest after their difficult trip. On August 9, Col. John Gibbon, with 200 troopers, attacked the sleeping camp at dawn. Once again, the Nez Perce were caught completely unaware; once again, their warriors launched a spirited counterattack. They put the Army on the defensive, which allowed the fugitives to pack up their belongings and flee. Nevertheless, close to 100 Nez Perce died in the savage fighting, most of them women, children, and the aged. Among the men with Gibbon, who was himself wounded, 30 were killed and 40 wounded. Only the timely arrival of Howard and his troops kept Gibbon from annihilation.

Before withdrawing, the Nez Perce buried their dead. Later, Howard allowed his Bannock Indian scouts to dig up, scalp, and mutilate the bodies. The news shocked and disgusted the Nez Perce, who throughout the ordeal had tried to follow the rules of civilized warfare, sparing civilian lives and tending to wounded enemies who fell into their hands.

The tragic odyssey of the Nez Perce ended on September 30 in the Bear Paw Mountains, less than 40 miles from the Canadian border. This time, soldiers under the command of Col. Nelson A. Miles surprised the fugitives. Again it was a near thing. Miles ordered a cavalry charge, but the soldiers had to cross 4 miles of open terrain, which gave the Nez Perce time to react.

White Bird set up a battle line of a hundred riflemen. They stopped the cavalry charge dead in its tracks, killing 24 troopers and wounding another 42. U.S. troopers managed to drive off most of the Nez Perce horses, so the Indians were trapped. Even worse, key warriors died in the initial attack, among them old Toohoolhoolzote and Ollokot, Joseph's brother, one of the best military minds in the Nez Perce camp. Surrounded by an overwhelming force armed with cannons, the fugitives had three choices: surrender, fight, or slip away during the night, leaving the elderly and wounded behind.

The Nez Perce were besieged for five days. During that time a storm blew in and heavy snow fell for two days, adding to their discomfort. Two Nez Perce treaty chiefs, accompanying the soldiers, entered the camp and tried to convince the fugitives to surrender, claiming that their people could return to Idaho homelands in the spring. Looking Glass and White Bird wanted to continue the fight; Joseph—worried about the women and children huddled in pits dug for protection from Nelson's howitzers—wanted to surrender. As the conference of chiefs broke up, a stray bullet struck Looking Glass in the head, killing him instantly. That night White Bird secretly led as many as 300 of the trapped Nez Perce through the military cordon and into Canada.

After four months and 1,700 miles, the end arrived for the Nez Perce. They fought and defeated several numerically superior armies; they behaved with dignity and restraint along the way; they committed few atrocities and paid for the supplies and ammunition they obtained from farmers and merchants. Embarrassed military commanders began to believe they were chasing a "Red Napoleon." But Napoleon himself could not have done much better, given the handicaps the fugitives faced.

Looking Glass joined Chief Joseph when soldiers attacked his reservation village. He suggested the bold plan of crossing the Lolo Trail into Montana to escape the Army. Knowing the trail well, he led the non-treaty bands in their desperate retreat.

Not only were the whites against them, but so were many of the tribes to whom they appealed for assistance. Indeed, warriors from several tribes joined the Army in the chase, attracted by the desire for fine Nez Perce horses as much as by the opportunity to earn war honors once again, even if on behalf of the white man.

On the afternoon of October 5, 1877, Joseph ended the struggle. "I am tired of fighting," he said. "Our chiefs are killed. Looking Glass is dead. Toohoolhoolzote is dead. The old men are all dead. It is the young men who say yes or no. He who led the young men [Joseph's brother, Ollokot] is dead. It is cold and we have no blankets. The little children are freezing to death. . . . Hear me my chiefs! I am tired. My heart is sick and sad. From where the sun now stands, I will fight no more forever." All the Nez Perce leaders deserve credit for the brilliant campaign, but when the end came, only Joseph was left, and he receives all the acclaim for the campaign.

These uncovered tepee poles stand at the site of the Big Hole battlefield in Montana, where pursuing troops surprised the Nez Perce refugees in their camp on August 9, 1877.

Joseph surrendered on the promise that he and his followers could return to Idaho. But the government ignored that promise and sent them instead to Oklahoma Territory. There they remained until 1883, when a few widows and orphans were allowed to return to Lapwai and the remaining Nez Perce Indians were sent with Joseph to the Colville reservation in northern Washington. None of Joseph's children went north with him. All had died in Oklahoma.

For the Nez Perce, these troubles had been a civil war, pitting family against family, band against band. The majority were already adjusting to the new order, so most did not suffer the psychological trauma that devastated their more militant neighbors on the Northern Plains. Like the Sioux, many Nez Perce—Joseph among them—sought an explanation and escape from their difficulties through dreamer religions. Their prayers, though, did not take the violent twist of the followers of the Ghost Dance, the dreamer religion that soon swept through the Sioux tribes in the late 1880s and raised suspicions among government officials, culminating in the massacre at Wounded Knee.

As for Joseph, for the rest of his life he pleaded to return to Idaho. The white people who lived in his former homeland objected, so he remained in Washington until his death in 1904. On the news of Joseph's death, an aide who had fought under General Howard wrote an appropriate epitaph: "I think that in his long career, Joseph cannot accuse the Government of the United States of one single act of justice."

RECORDING THE STORIES

✳

Not all Indians spoke so eloquently in public as did Chief Joseph. Others moved silently onto the reservation, their memories full. Thomas B. Marquis, a physician from Seattle, Washington, became so fascinated with the stories known by Indian elders that he gave up his practice, moved onto a reservation in southeastern Montana, and spent several decades befriending the aged Crow and Cheyenne people who lived there. Those meetings resulted in images and testimonies that would otherwise have been lost to history.

The elderly Indians learned to trust their kind white friend. He cared for them as well as interviewed them, giving them food, money, and medical care when they needed it. At a time when many Indians would have nothing to do with white people, these elders spoke honestly and freely with Dr. Marquis. "I held out continual invitations for Custer battle veteran warriors to visit my home, partake of my food, and smoke my tobacco," Marquis recalled. "After a long siege, they began to come. Later they began to talk."

Marquis eventually became adept enough at sign language that he seldom needed an interpreter. In addition to collecting their stories and taking their pictures, Marquis obtained guns and other relics of the Indian wars from his informants, now part of the museum collection at the Little Bighorn Battlefield National Monument. Marquis died in 1935, at the age of 66.

When Thomas B. Marquis interviewed Iron Teeth, a Northern Cheyenne survivor, she was 92 years old. She cherished a hide scraper made from the horn of an elk. "When I die," she told Marquis, "this gift from my husband must be buried with me."

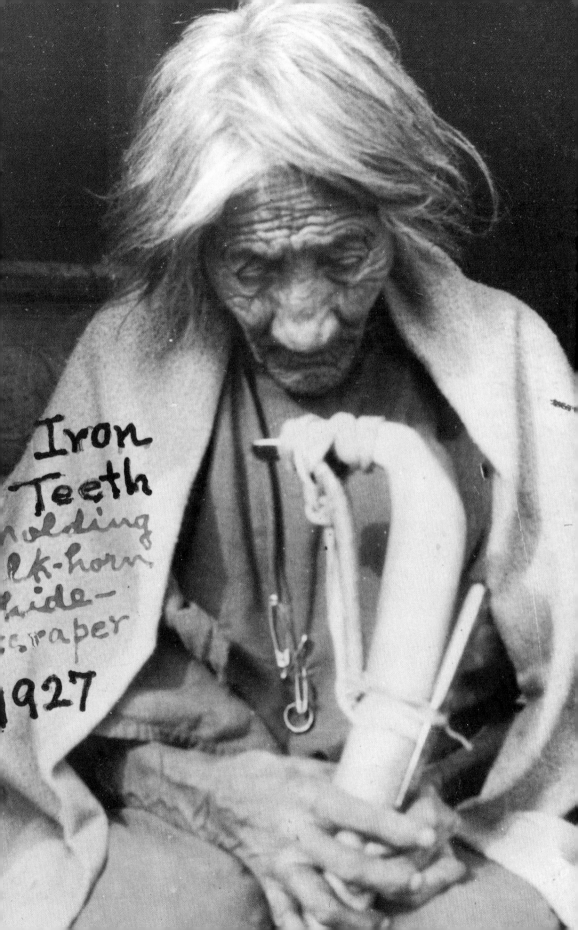

Iron
Teeth
holding
elk-horn
hide—
scraper
1927

Wooden Leg

Thomas Marquis's favorite informant was Wooden Leg, right. After extensive interviews, Marquis wrote Wooden Leg's life story, *A Warrior Who Fought Custer.* Marquis interviewed many other veterans of the Battle of the Little Bighorn, including *Phillip Rising Sun* (below), along with his father, Iron Shirt, his son, Wolf, and his grandson, Medicine Bull.

4 generations in male line

Iron Shirt 96   Rising Sun 68   Wolf? 40   Medicine Bull 6

1927

Dr. T. B. M.

Custer battle veteran Two Feathers 1927

Thomas Marquis also operated a little museum in Hardin, Montana, adjoining the Crow Indian Reservation, where he displayed Seventh Cavalry items salvaged by Indians after the Battle of the Little Bighorn, such as the Springfield carbine proudly held by Two Feathers.

"I have found what I was after. This is my last day
on earth. Often I have thought of my dead father
and have wondered how I could get to him.
Now I see the way."

— BLACK HORSE, RAIDING
A WHITE MAN'S FARM IN SEARCH OF HORSES

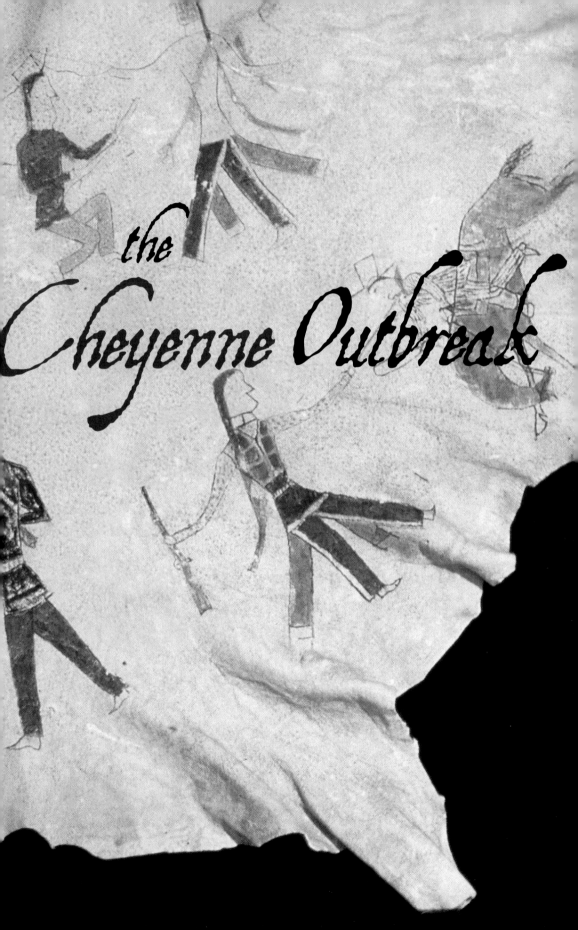

Turn-of-the-20th-century photographer Edward S. Curtis excelled in evoking images of a romantic, rapidly disappearing way of life, such as this scene of mounted Plains warriors scanning a distant landscape.

1879

✳

The words of Chief Joseph echoed through the American conscious-
ness, a counterpoint to the blows suffered in 1876. The Battle of the
Little Bighorn had shocked a nation enjoying its centennial year: Not
only had George Armstrong Custer died, but so had his brothers Tom
and Boston, his nephew, Autie Reed, and his brother-in-law, Lt. James
Calhoun. The impact on the American public of their loss is best likened
to the Kennedy assassinations a century later. The Custer brothers were
so beloved and therefore grieved that no one talked peace with the Indians any longer. Within a year, all the Indians who had been camping
along the Little Bighorn on that fateful day in June 1876 were either
dead, on reservations, or in Canada with Sitting Bull.

Crazy Horse surrendered in May 1877. Exhausted from constant
pursuit, his people near starving, he arrived at Camp Robinson in north-
western Nebraska, near the Red Cloud Agency. Eight hundred followers rode in procession with him, armed, painted, and singing war songs.
Four months later, Crazy Horse was stabbed to death while resisting arrest
at the agency—at least that was how government officials explained it.
"It is good," one of his saddened followers remarked. "Crazy Horse has
looked for death and it has come."

Perhaps the cruelest fate, though, had befallen the Northern
Cheyenne, attacked by some one thousand cavalrymen while in their
winter camp. The soldiers had driven them from their village, then
destroyed their tepees, clothing, and food supply. That one night, 11
Cheyenne babies had frozen to death. The survivors had eventually found
shelter with Crazy Horse, and they were with him when he surrendered. Instead of placing them on a reservation on their own Northern
Plains, the Bureau of Indian Affairs transferred the entire village—some
thousand men, women, and children—a thousand miles south to the
Cheyenne and Arapaho agency at Darlington, in Oklahoma.

Unable to adapt to the intense heat in their new home, demor-
alized and despondent, the Northern Cheyenne sickened and died in

PRECEDING PAGES: *This Cheyenne hide painting depicts tribal wars between*
the Cheyenne and the Crow.

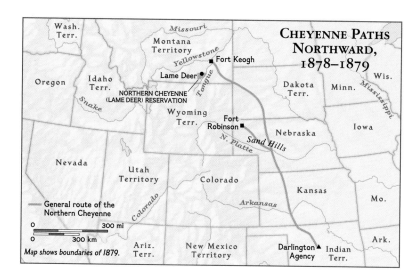

CHEYENNE PATHS
NORTHWARD,
1878–1879

General route of the
Northern Cheyenne

0   300 mi

0   300 km

Map shows boundaries of 1879.

appalling numbers. "In Oklahoma we all got sick with chills and fever," recalled Iron Teeth, the elderly Cheyenne woman who told Thomas Marquis her story in 1927. "When we were not sick we were hungry." After a year of suffering, their pleas to go home ignored, the despondent Cheyenne began urging their leaders, Dull Knife and Little Wolf, to seize the initiative. They thought they should simply sneak away from Darlington and make their way back north, even though it was a journey of more than a thousand miles. No matter that they lacked weapons, horses, and equipment: It was better to die in battle than to waste away without dignity or pride.

One of the agitators was Black Horse, who had already been shot at Darlington in 1875 while resisting arrest. In the late summer of 1878, he and two friends, Mad Hearted Wolf and Whetstone, left Darlington and headed north. The Indian agent ordered Dull Knife to bring the renegades back. Knowing this would be impossible, and fearful that the Army would punish everyone for the transgression, Dull Knife and Little Wolf led some 300 Northern Cheyenne, fewer than 90 of them warriors, on one of the most remarkable odysseys in American history. They packed their few belongings and took off from Darlington on September 9, 1878.

The runaway strategy was to split up into several groups, each wending its separate way toward the Tongue River in present-day Montana. Eventually the groups came together, rejoining Black Horse and his companions as well. Although the chiefs had urged their people not to harm any whites they encountered, violence was inevitable, since the Indians needed horses.

Black Horse excelled in capturing horses. As the main party traveled through the Sand Hills of northern Nebraska, he and two or three companions would break off, sometimes on foot but sometimes on worn-out horses that they hoped to replace. One reason Black Horse so willingly took these risks, he later explained, was to atone for the harm he and his companions had caused in leaving Darlington. "We three had better go to war," one of his companions pointed out. "We shall have to bear the blame of everything that has happened along the way, for we three were the first ones to leave the Southern agency to come up here. We are in for it, and we may as well carry it out. We may as well do as much as we can before we are caught."

Black Horse and his companions sought white men to fight. To kill one would be a great achievement—a coup, a war honor. During one horse-hunting raid, Black Horse noticed a white man coming their way. "One of our 'friends' is coming," he told the others. The warriors knelt in ambush, then all fired at once. When the horse fell, pinning the rider to the ground, Black Horse and the others rushed forward, counted coup, and killed their hapless victim. It was one of the most successful raids during the flight: they captured a hundred head of horses from nearby ranches, enough to provide fresh mounts for everyone who needed one.

The Cheyenne eluded their pursuers on the long trek from Oklahoma to Montana. The horse and travois—shown below in an 1889 photograph of a Cheyenne family— allowed them to travel lightly and quickly.

FOLLOWING PAGES: Storm clouds gather over the Central Plains.

out and fight the soldiers. They will kill me, but they will think I am the only one here, and they will go away after I am dead. When they are gone, you can come out and hunt for our mother." The next day, she dared to venture from the cave. Soldiers captured her, but she was eventually reunited with her mother.

Thanks to Thomas Marquis, we have Iron Teeth's story. "Lots of times," she told him, "as I sit here alone on the floor with my blanket wrapped about me, I lean forward and close my eyes and think of him . . . fighting the soldiers, knowing that he would be killed, but doing this so his little sister might get away in safety. Don't you think he was a brave young man?"

Soldiers from Fort Robinson survey slain Cheyenne in this painting by Frederic Remington. The Army sent the Indians' skeletons to the Smithsonian Institution. In 1993, the remains were repatriated and buried on the Northern Cheyenne Reservation in Montana. "All they wanted to do is go home, and now they can," said tribal chairman Levando Fisher.

The Cheyenne remaining with Little Wolf, including Black Horse hid in the Nebraska Sand Hills until March and then, when the weather improved, continued north. When they reached present-day Montana, they met several Northern Cheyenne operating out of Fort Keogh as scouts for the U.S. cavalry. One was Wolf-Voice, a Gros Ventre who had married into the Cheyenne tribe. He said that Lt. W. P. Clark—known as White Hat to the Cheyenne and a friend of Little Wolf—hoped the runaways would surrender without a fight. If they did so, Clark thought he could prevail on the federal government to let them stay in the north country. Little Wolf accepted the offer, and the next day the Cheyenne met with Clark, one of the minority of soldiers on the western frontier

FOLLOWING PAGES: Snow sifts over miles of Wyoming flatlands, an empty scene of silence save for two mule deer. A landscape like this looked more like home to the Northern Cheyenne than that of the reservation near Darlington, Oklahoma, to which they were ordered by U.S. authorities.

sympathetic to the plight of the American Indians at that time. With Clark was an Army doctor, who attended to the sick and wounded Cheyenne, including Black Horse. Little Wolf surrendered in March 1879, bringing with him 33 men, 43 women, and 38 children— a pitiful remnant of the 300 Northern Cheyenne who had left Darlington the previous October.

Little Wolf, at left, and Dull Knife, also known as Morning Star, led their followers from Oklahoma to Montana in 1878. Today the Northern Cheyenne venerate them for the ordeal they underwent so that their homeland would be restored.

Lieutenant Clark kept his word. Little Wolf's people were allowed to remain in their northern homeland. Shortly thereafter, the federal government created for the Northern Cheyenne a reservation in the rolling hills and rich grasslands near the Tongue River. There, at last, the surviving followers of Little Wolf and Dull Knife settled, together with several other Cheyenne bands that had not been sent to Oklahoma. The reservation is often called Lame Deer, after its principal town, named for a Lakota chief who died nearby in a fight with the U.S. Cavalry.

Wooden Leg, Iron Teeth, Black Horse, and the other Cheyenne survivors of the Indian wars lived out the rest of their lives on the Lame Deer reservation. Most of the men—among them Black Horse, whose shattered leg left him lame for the rest of his life—enlisted as scouts in the U.S. Cavalry under Clark. Sometimes they told their stories to the few white people who befriended them: Dr. Marquis, who gave the old ones free medical care, and George Bird Grinnell, the noted ethnologist whose classic work, *The Cheyenne Indians,* published in 1923, drew significantly from his conversations with elders at Lame Deer. Of Black Horse, Grinnell wrote that the "elderly and crippled warrior . . . was a great fighter in the decade between 1870 and 1880."

The Cheyenne escape from Oklahoma and the massacre at Fort Robinson marked the last poignant moments in the Indian wars of the Northern Plains. For these proud warrior peoples, a new era had arrived. They were destined to become, in fact and in idiom, vanishing Americans, their numbers dwindling, their cultures forgotten. The brutal and bloody struggles they had had to wage to defend their way of life had left them an embittered people, living in economic poverty, under tremendous cultural stress, on barren and isolated reservations. Where once they had roamed freely across the Northern Plains, they were now forced into a way of life they could not understand or would not accept. The ingredients were all there, festering for more than a decade until another cataclysmic outbreak erupted in 1890 at Wounded Knee. ↰

GHOST DANCE

✴

The Ghost Dance religion originated in 1889 with the prophet Wovoka. He believed that Indians could attain paradise if they lived peaceful, industrious lives and performed a special dance. Lakota emissaries turned his message militant: If Indians everywhere practiced the Ghost Dance, whites would disappear, dead Indians would revive, and the buffalo would return. Soon many Lakota were believers.

The Ghost Dance ceremony usually began around noon. After eating food that had been blessed, the dancers—male and female, young and old—would join hands and sing and dance together, circling a tree. Their songs evoked the old way of life, as does this one, recorded by Smithsonian ethnologist James Mooney:

> *The whole world is coming,*
> *A nation is coming, a nation is coming,*
> *The eagle has brought the message to the tribe.*
> *The father says so, the father says so.*
> *Over the whole earth they are coming,*
> *The buffalo are coming, the buffalo are coming,*
> *The crow has brought the message to the tribe,*
> *The father says so, the father says so.*

The dance started slowly and softly, but the tempo and volume soon increased. Some dancers became dizzy, trembled and stumbled, then fell unconscious to the ground. Thus entranced, a person's spirit soared to paradise and greeted dead relatives and friends. Those who failed to faint eagerly waited for others to awaken and tell tales from the spirit world that they had just visited.

Paiute Indian and Ghost Dance prophet Wovoka, also known as Jack Wilson, claimed that while lying delirious with fever during a solar eclipse in January 1889, he visited heaven, spoke with God, and saw departed Indians living in peace and happiness.

As a priest paints and blesses two men, preparing them for the Ghost Dance, women sing and dance with arms upraised. Smithsonian ethnologist James Mooney took these photographs on an Arapaho reservation in Oklahoma in 1891. Apparently the Arapaho did not feel threatened by his presence.

"You must make a dance to continue five days," the prophet Wovoka had revealed. Ghost dancers kept moving four nights running. The fifth night, they danced until morning, then bathed in the river and went home, according to a Cheyenne account in 1891.

"You ask me to plow the ground!
Shall I take a knife and tear my mother's bosom?"

— SMOHALLA, A LEADER OF ONE OF THE DREAMER RELIGIONS

Big Foot, a Miniconjou chief, went as a delegate to Washington in 1888 and slept in an Army tent at Wounded Knee in 1890, but he was among the first to be killed there.

1890

✳

After the Battle of the Little Bighorn, the U.S. Army had been so relentless in its pursuit of Sitting Bull's followers that by the end of 1877, the only survivors were either on reservations or in Canada, where some 2,000 of them had fled, seeking the protection of the Great Grandmother while hoping to escape the wrath of the Great Father. But life was lonely and hard there. As the buffalo disappeared and hunger became a constant companion, the refugees slowly and quietly began returning to friends and families south of the border. Band by band, the families and followers of Spotted Eagle, Rain-in-the-Face, Black Moon, Crow King, Gall, Little Hawk, and Low Dog left the land of the Great Grandmother. In July 1881 the remaining diehards, Sitting Bull and fewer than 40 families—44 men, 143 women and children, starving, wearing threadbare clothes, and in possession of only 14 gaunt ponies—arrived at Fort Buford, just 50 miles south of the Canada border in today's North Dakota. "I wish it to be remembered," the weary chief said, "that I was the last man of my tribe to surrender my rifle."

Sitting Bull's resignation marked a turning point in the history of the American Indian. Another came five years later, when Geronimo and his handful of followers turned in their rifles for the last time in Skeleton Canyon, Arizona, on September 4, 1886. The conquest was nearly complete. The United States government, having defeated the Western tribes militarily, next attempted to defeat them politically and spiritually.

Allied with powerful Eastern church groups and self-proclaimed humanitarian organizations, the government launched a massive campaign to assimilate the Indians into white society. The only way to accomplish this, the humanitarians believed, was to transform tribal society and eradicate native religions. Simply put, the humanitarian credo was: "To reach the full-blooded Indian, send after him a full-blooded Christian farmer." The reformers naively believed that the concept of private property and individual land ownership at the heart of their civilization would be incentive enough for Indians to adopt all the other trappings of white life.

PRECEDING PAGES: *In 1990, a century after the Lakota rode unaware to Wounded Knee, 200 Indians retraced the route "to wipe away the tears."*

Members of Big Foot's Miniconjou Lakota band, opposite, assemble for a dance in August 1890 on the Cheyenne River Reservation in South Dakota. The man at the far right is wearing a Ghost Shirt, made from the cloth sacks in which the Indians received their flour rations from the government.

The goal was to turn Indians into land-owning farmers by giving each of them an allotment—160 acres of tribal lands to each head of family.

Allotments had been attempted—and failed—on a minor scale as early as the 1850s. Their advocates insisted that the program could be made to work with modifications and guarantees, so during the 1880s, the call for allotments crescendoed, linking both Eastern and Western interests. Western whites welcomed the program because, after allotments were assigned, the surplus lands once belonging to individual tribes would be sold to whites for settlement.

Defeated, dispirited, trapped between two worlds, the Western tribes did, in fact, turn to religion to escape their psychological holocaust—but the religions that comforted them were nativist, not Christian. Three culture-reviving prophets burst upon the scene in the closing years of the 19th century. Whites called them "dreamers" because their religions were based on trance-induced experiences with the spirit world.

Two of the dreamers—Smohalla, a Wanapum, and Skolaskin, a Sans Poil—lived within 300 miles of each other, along the Columbia River in the plateau country of the Pacific Northwest. Both preached a message combining elements of Christianity with native beliefs and stressing adherence to traditional ways, as epitomized in a speech by Smohalla: "You ask me to plow the ground! Shall I take a knife and tear my mother's bosom? Then when I die she will not take me to her bosom to rest. . . . You ask me to cut grass and make hay and sell it, and be rich like white men! But how dare I cut off my mother's hair?" The dreamers gained national attention when Chief Joseph announced that he and his band were believers. Dreamer religions remained popular until well into the 1890s and spawned numerous other sects in the Northwest, such as the Indian Shaker Church, founded in 1881.

*M*ore influential and widespread by far was the Ghost Dance, the third nativist religion founded at the close of the 19th century. Its prophet was Wovoka, a Paiute, but his message was swiftly adopted by the Lakota, who needed little urging to take up a religious practice that gave them reasons for hope. It is difficult for us today to appreciate their trauma, living on desolate tracts of land, under constant cultural stress, enduring economic and emotional poverty. No longer could they hunt buffalo or practice their religion. Instead they were to become farmers and send their children to school to become educated Christians. They depended on government rations, slim to start and further reduced when

a tribal census showed their population smaller than expected. The disastrous winter of 1886 killed off some 30 percent of their cattle. The summer of 1890 set drought and heat records. "The Sioux country in that year was a veritable dust bowl," wrote Elaine Goodale, a white reservation teacher who saw "pitiful little gardens" and "heartbroken mothers [who] mourned the last of a series of dead babies." Is it any wonder that these proud people would grasp at anything that offered hope?

As the Ghost Dance religion spread, reservation agents viewed it as a threat to their authority and a sign of impending conflict. Many Indian agents were products of the patronage system at its worst: inexperienced, ineffectual, and ill equipped for such a crisis. Typical was Daniel F. Royer, the agent at Pine Ridge, called Young-Man-Afraid-of-Indians by the Lakota. When Ghost Dancers defied him on November 15, 1890, Royer telegraphed the Commissioner of Indian Affairs, saying, "Indians are dancing in the snow and are wild and crazy. . . . We need protection and we need it now."

Five days later, several units of U.S. Infantry and Cavalry rattled onto the Pine Ridge and Rosebud Reservations, equipped with Hotchkiss rapid-fire cannons and Gatling guns. Rather than restoring order, the soldiers raised the threshold of hysteria. Large numbers of Ghost Dance

FOLLOWING PAGES:
Many Plains Indians
joined the Ghost Dance,
looking to the heavens
as life on earth felt
more and more hopeless.

Sitting Bull appeared in Buffalo Bill's Wild West Show in 1885, the same year Annie Oakley joined. The old Indian chief earned $50 a week for four months, plus a signing bonus of $125. He further negotiated two weeks' advance pay and the sole right to sell his autograph.

believers fled to the Badlands, in the northwest corner of the Pine Ridge Reservation, and threw themselves into a frenzy of dancing.

Meanwhile, attention turned to Sitting Bull, now living north of Pine Ridge on the Standing Rock Reservation. After returning from Canada in July 1881, he had been a prisoner of the U.S. government for two years at Fort Randall in the Dakota Territory. From there, in May 1883, he was transferred to Standing Rock. The Indian agent there, Maj. James McLaughlin, began receiving requests from entrepreneurs who wished to take Sitting Bull on tour. Typical of the petitioners, a clergyman from Jamestown, Dakota, wanted Sitting Bull at his church fair.

McLaughlin worried that tours would feed Sitting Bull's already inflated ego, but he permitted two of them. One, organized by his own friends, visited 25 cities in the fall of 1884 but failed financially. More successful was the tour the following year with William F. Cody's celebrated Wild West Show. Sitting Bull was an instant success, and he got along fabulously with Cody, better known as Buffalo Bill. A photograph captioned "Enemies in '76, Friends in '85," taken in Montreal, was part of the publicity campaign. Sitting Bull rode in parades, greeted visitors, and signed autographs, but he did not participate in the sham battles of the Wild West Show. When the tour ended, Cody gave Sitting Bull a large white sombrero and the light gray circus horse he had ridden in the arena—possessions he cherished up to his death four years later.

All in all, it was a positive experience for the bitter old man. He showered money on street urchins and helped the roustabouts erect the big top, matching them swing for swing with a sledgehammer. He was fascinated by Annie Oakley and called her *Wan-tan-yeya ci-sci-la,* which translates roughly as Little Sure Shot. He even tried to adopt her. When the old chief got moody or irritable—a frequent occurrence—Annie could get him to smile by skipping through her little dance routine.

Reservation life still held no appeal for Sitting Bull, and he was in constant conflict with McLaughlin. The old chief had many demands, and the agent considered him an obstacle to his people's progress. So when Sitting Bull threatened to join the Ghost Dancers, McLaughlin decided to have him arrested. Before dawn on December 15, 1890, 40 Indian policemen approached Sitting Bull's camp on the Grand River, about 30 miles from Fort Yates on the Standing Rock Reservation.

At first light, two of the policemen brought the chief's gray horse to the front of his cabin. Several others slammed open the door, calling out, "We have come to arrest you." Sitting Bull, awakened from a sound sleep, was groggy and confused. The policemen tried to place him on his horse. A crowd began to gather, alerted by the sounds of the police, the barking of dogs, and the shrieks of Sitting Bull's wife. The Indians began to yell, "Let him go! Protect our chief!"

Sitting Bull appeared dazed. His young son, Crow Foot, stood in the cabin doorway and started to berate him: "You always called yourself a brave chief. Now you are allowing yourself to be taken by the metal breasts." Sitting Bull pulled back, and someone shot one of the policemen holding onto him. As the policeman fell, he shot Sitting Bull.

Bullets began flying in every direction. When it was over, Sitting Bull, Crow Foot, seven of Sitting Bull's followers, and six policemen

FOLLOWING PAGES:
In 1890 Ghost Dance leaders Two Strike and Crow Dog led more than a thousand followers into the Badlands. When tensions eased, they returned and camped near the Pine Ridge Agency. News of Wounded Knee fomented revenge, but these two leaders sought to end the violence and surrendered on January 15, 1891.

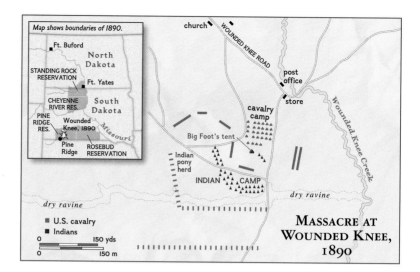

Map shows boundaries of 1890.

Ft. Buford

North Dakota

STANDING ROCK RESERVATION

Ft. Yates

CHEYENNE RIVER RES.

South Dakota

PINE RIDGE. RES.

Wounded Knee, 1890

Missouri

Pine Ridge

ROSEBUD RESERVATION

church

WOUNDED KNEE ROAD

post office

store

cavalry camp

Big Foot's tent

Wounded Knee Creek

Indian pony herd

INDIAN ▲▲▲ CAMP

dry ravine

dry ravine

■ U.S. cavalry
■ Indians

0   150 yds
0   150 m

MASSACRE AT WOUNDED KNEE, 1890

had died. During all this, the chief's circus horse, imagining itself back in the Wild West Show, sat on its haunches and went through its routine, waving a hoof in the air as though shaking hands. Indian observers believed that the spirit of the slain chief had entered his horse.

*O*nce again the government had overreacted. Even before the attempted arrest of Sitting Bull, disillusioned Ghost Dancers had been returning to their agencies, the threat of starvation and the onset of winter eroding their militancy. By the end of December all were coming back, even the followers of Chief Big Foot (also known as Spotted Elk), some of the most fervent believers. Big Foot's band numbered about 350 men, women, and children, joined by some 40 Hunkpapa after the death of Sitting Bull. All were cold and hungry. Big Foot, gravely ill with pneumonia, was so weak he rode in the back of a wagon.

Less than 30 miles from the Pine Ridge Agency, the forlorn Ghost Dancers encountered four troops of the Seventh Cavalry, Custer's old outfit. In fact, several of the officers who had fought at the Little Bighorn still remained with the Seventh. Uncertain what to do, the soldiers escorted the Indians to their camp on Wounded Knee Creek, where they gave Big Foot a large Army tent and a camp stove and made him as comfortable as possible. The Indians offered no resistance, but the commanding officer still decided to disarm them in the morning.

So Big Foot's followers arose to find themselves in the middle of a military park. Surrounding them were 500 soldiers and a battery of four Hotchkiss cannons, which could fire 50 explosive two-inch shells a minute.

The Indian men were told to assemble in front of Big Foot's tent and turn over their guns. The order angered and frightened the men, who feared that the soldiers would kill them once they disarmed. They produced only a few old guns. Squads of soldiers began searching their tents for additional weapons, while other troops prepared to search the men, who remained seated in a group, blankets clutched tightly about them. An already tense situation was made worse by Yellow Bird, a medicine man and staunch Ghost Dancer. "Do not be afraid," he told the anxious warriors, many of whom were wearing their sacred shirts. "I have assurance that the soldier bullets cannot penetrate us; the prairie is large and the bullets will not go toward you; they will not penetrate us."

A deaf Indian named Black Coyote ("a crazy man, a young man of very bad influence and in fact a nobody," one Indian recounted) began muttering and walking about, waving his rifle, then yelling, "This gun belongs to me. I have paid much money for it." Two soldiers struggled to take his gun away, and it discharged. At that instant Yellow Bird threw some dirt into the air. Whether they considered it a signal or not, several young men jumped up, threw aside their blankets, and leveled their Winchester rifles at the nearest squad of soldiers.

A blinding snowstorm at Wounded Knee delayed burials for three days. A Nebraska photographer visited the site. His chilling series of photographs documents the carnage. Big Foot's village had been swept by cannon fire; hot shells had set fire to the tents. Some of the snow mounds and dark objects are dead bodies.

Birds Eye View of Battle Field at Wounded Knee S.D. looking North

The surrounding soldiers opened fire. Fully half the Indian men fell at the first volley. The rest charged the soldiers, but after minutes of fighting with knives and tomahawks, most turned and ran toward the tents and their families. Hotchkiss cannons began raining explosive shells at them. The artillerymen later claimed they tried to avoid harming women and children, but it was almost impossible to sort them out in the melee. When warriors including Yellow Bird took refuge in the village and began shooting, the artillerymen reduced the tents to skeletons. The focus then shifted to a nearby ravine, where Indian survivors—men, women, and children—were seeking shelter. The artillerymen raked this area with cannons, too. A few Indians tried to resist, but most simply ran until they collapsed from exhaustion or wounds.

The shooting stopped around noon. Fifty-one wounded Indians were taken to Pine Ridge, where seven died. After the soldiers left, many more dead and wounded were taken from the battlefield. The soldiers counted twenty-five officers and enlisted men dead—some of them killed in the crossfire by their own bullets—and about forty wounded. One soldier, already injured, died at the hands of a badly wounded Indian woman who crawled from the village with a butcher knife clutched in her teeth. As she stabbed him, another soldier shot her.

The exact death toll will never be known. A blizzard blew up soon after the confrontation, so it was New Year's Day, three days later, when the Army finally returned to Wounded Knee to bury the Indian dead. The burial party interred 146 Indians on the battlefield—84 men and boys, 44 women, and 18 children. With the burial party was Charles Eastman, the physician at Pine Ridge, who was himself a Santee Sioux. The first body they found was of a woman lying under the snow a full three miles from the scene of the fighting. "From this point on," Eastman recalled, "we found them scattered along as [if] they had been relentlessly hunted down and slaughtered while fleeing for their lives."

Far worse was the sight awaiting them at the Indians' camp: scraps of burned canvas clinging to charred tent poles, scattered belongings and bedding, and mounds of snow, each hiding one or more hapless victims. "It took all my nerve to keep my composure in the face of this spectacle, and of the excitement and grief of my Indian companions, nearly every one of whom was crying aloud or singing his death song," Eastman remembered. It was, he later confessed, "a severe ordeal for one who had so lately put all his faith in the Christian love and lofty ideals of the white man."

Incredibly, the burial party found several half-frozen survivors, including two infants who been shielded from the elements by their

Miniconjou Chief Big Foot lies dead in the snow of Wounded Knee. Behind his body stands the charred frame of the tent and stove given to him by soldiers to help keep him warm. Soldiers had carried the ailing chief from his tent, expecting him to tell his warriors to surrender their weapons. He refused to do so. In these tense moments, violence erupted. Big Foot was one of the first to die.

THE MASSACRE AT WOUNDED KNEE

mothers' bodies. One of the infant survivors, a girl, was wearing a buckskin cap decorated with a beaded American flag. She was later adopted by Brig. Gen. Leonard W. Colby, who named her Marguerite—but the Indian women at Pine Ridge called her "Lost Bird" and "Child of the Battlefield." Blue Whirlwind received 14 shrapnel wounds from a Hotchkiss cannon shell, but she survived, along with two young sons, also wounded, at her side. All three had lived through the blizzard and three days without food or shelter.

More than a century has passed since that day in 1890, yet the fascination with the massacre near Wounded Knee Creek still stays strong. Historians still debate its causes and significance. Some have accused the Indians of plotting a murderous assault on their captors; others have condemned the Army for a needless atrocity. Neither position is correct, of course: If fault lay anywhere, it was in the decision to disarm the Indians. Already tense, fearful of Army intentions, and at the same time confident of the spiritual power in their Ghost Shirts, the warriors needed little encouragement to fight back.

FOLLOWING PAGES: The cultures, character, stories, and values of the Plains Indians may have faded with the end of the Indian wars in 1890, but they did not disappear. Like this tepee in a Rocky Mountain snowstorm, they remain—a constant force in our American heritage.

Wounded Knee was an instant media event, thanks to nearby reporters including Frederic Remington, the famous reporter-artist for *Harper's Weekly*. Twenty miles away, at the Pine Ridge Agency, where it was thought the real action would take place, Remington missed the conflict. He published sketches based on U.S. Cavalry eyewitness accounts, one of which gave the impression that they were the victims.

A Northern Plains shield like this one, made of thick buffalo hide, could stop an arrow. Its real power came, the Indians believed, from the medicine paintings on it and the blessings given when it was made.

The photographic record of Wounded Knee has likewise seared this event forever as a landmark in American Indian history. Because of those pictures—taken by a photographer from Chadron, Nebraska, who joined the burial detail at the killing field on New Year's Day—Wounded Knee has an immediacy and permanence that will forever scar the American conscience. The sight of Big Foot lying dead in the snow, and the others who perished with him, has haunted Americans ever since.

Most writers consider Wounded Knee the last battle of the Indian wars, but in fact they had ended with Geronimo's surrender in 1886. Wounded Knee was not a battle, either: It was an emotional outburst. Neither side wanted bloodshed, but once it started, it was impossible to stop. The U.S. soldiers had cannons and Big Foot's followers had a handful of rifles and pistols, knives and tomahawks, so the event at Wounded Knee was more a massacre than a battle—a sad footnote to the valiant American Indian effort in the West to hold the white man at bay.

Through the second half of the 19th century, the Indians had fought hard and well. But the conflict over the lands of the West was one they were destined to lose as their homeland was overwhelmed by the floods of European immigration and United States expansion. Although they had lost the armed conflict for land, the wars continued—fought on cultural and political fronts and against new foes: humanitarians, educators, bureaucrats, and speculators. In a sense, today's American Indians have finally won those wars, thanks to their ability to adapt to new times and new challenges while keeping alive ancient and unbroken traditions that have sustained them for thousands of years.

Wounded Knee has become, in fact and symbol, the measure marking 1890 as the end of 400 years of armed conflict between Native American tribes and white newcomers for control of the lands of North America. Interestingly, 1890 is also the year that a young historian named Frederick Jackson Turner noted that, for the first time ever, the U.S. census failed to identify any lands free of white settlement in the West. Articulating the concept that led to his becoming a major historian of his day, Turner announced the official end of the American frontier. ↰

The whole world is coming,
A nation is coming,
The eagle has brought the message
to the tribe.

— GHOST DANCE SONG

ABOUT THE AUTHOR

Herman J. Viola, a curator emeritus of the Smithsonian Institution and former director of the National Anthropological Archives, started a training program for American Indian historians at the Smithsonian in 1972. Through this program he befriended numerous Indian scholars, like Dr. George P. Horse Capture, who wrote the introduction to this book; Dr. Joseph Medicine Crow, grandson to White Man Runs Him, one of Custer's six Crow scouts; and Senator Ben Nighthorse Campbell, great-grandson to Black Horse, a prominent Cheyenne warrior. These friendships gave Dr. Viola unique access to the Indian community. He collected family stories of the Indian wars and the early reservation days, some of which are included in this book. Dr. Viola is the author of numerous books on American Indian topics, including *Ben Nighthorse Campbell: An American Warrior, Little Bighorn Remembered, Warrior Artists, After Columbus,* and *It Is a Good Day to Die.* A consultant to the National Museum of the American Indian, a lecturer, and a teacher, Dr. Viola lives in Falls Church, Virginia, with his wife, Susan.

ACKNOWLEDGMENTS

Publication of this book was a team effort, and what a team the Book Division of the National Geographic Society assembled. I am especially grateful to Barbara Brownell-Grogan and Dale Herring, who originated the idea for the book and then selected me to write it. Special thanks also go to Susan Tyler Hitchcock, who gets credit for the crispness of the text. I also want to thank Trudy Pearson, the picture researcher, Cinda Rose, the designer, and Eleanor Stables, the researcher, for their excellent work. I am thankful for my friends in the Indian community who have enriched my life by allowing me to become a part of theirs, especially George P. Horse Capture. Thank you, George, for the thoughtful and heartfelt introduction. Finally, I want to thank my wife, Susan, who shares with me my love of history, books, and the American West.

—Herman J. Viola

ADDITIONAL READING

Andrist, Ralph K. *The Long Death: The Last Days of the Plains Indian.* New York: The Macmillan Co., 1964.

Marquis, Thomas B. *The Cheyennes of Montana.* Introduction and Biography of the Author by Thomas D. Weist. Algonac, Mich.: Reference Publications, 1978.

_____. *Keep the Last Bullet for Yourself: The True Story of Custer's Last Stand.* Introduction by Joseph Medicine Crow. Algonac, Mich.: Reference Publications, 1976.

Powell, Peter John. *People of the Sacred Mountain: A History of the Northern Cheyenne Chiefs and Warrior Societies, 1830-1879, with an Epilogue, 1969-1974.* 2 vols. San Francisco: Harper & Row, Publishers, 1979.

Utley, Robert M. *The Indian Frontier of the American West, 1846-1890.* Lincoln: U. of Nebraska Press, 1984.

Viola, Herman J. *After Columbus: The Smithsonian Chronicle of the North American Indians.* Washington, D.C.: The Smithsonian Institution Press, 1990.

_____. *Ben Nighthorse Campbell: An American Warrior.* New York: Orion Books, 1993.

_____. *Diplomats in Buckskins: A History of Indian Delegations in Washington City.* Washington, D.C.: The Smithsonian Institution Press, 1981.

_____. *Lincoln and the Indians.* Madison, Wisc.: Lincoln Fellowship of Wisconsin, Bulletin 31, 1975.

_____. *Little Bighorn Remembered: The Untold Indian Story of Custer's Last Stand.* New York: Times Books, 1999.

_____. *Warrior Artists: Historic Cheyenne and Kiowa Indian Ledger Art Drawn by Making Medicine and Zotom.* Washington, D.C.: National Geographic Society, 1998.

ILLUSTRATION CREDITS

Michael Sample/Danita Delimont, Agent, 1, 2-3, 68-69, 142-143; National Museum of American Art, Washington, DC/Art Resource, 4-5; Nebraska State Historical Society, 6; Amon Carter Museum, Fort Worth, Texas, 10-11; Courtesy National Archives and Records Administration, 13, 36-37, 113, 134 (Neg. 87743), 147 (Neg. 87744), 159, 164-65; Smithsonian Institution 16-17, 18, 21, 29, 30, 33, 35, 38-39 (background), 38-39, 42, 55, 58-59, 60, 75, 80, 92-93, 94 (photo by Henry Hird III), 99, 106 (Glen Swanson Collection), 112, 122, 123, 128 (Glen Swanson Collection), 129 (lower), 130-131, 151, 152, 152-153, 153, 171, 174, 175, 178, 181, 186-187, 189, 191, 195; Michael Forsberg/Danita Delimont, Agent, 22-23; Mark R. Godfrey, 24, 160-162; Minnesota Historical Society, 25; Courtesy Mr. & Mrs. Norris Jones, 26; CORBIS (background image), 34, 36-37, 38-39, 54, 56-57, 74, 76-77, 100, 102-103, 126, 128-129, 130-131, 150, 152-153, 172-173, 174-175: Colorado Historical Society, 40-41; Southern Methodist University, 44; Colorado Historical Society, 45, 49; Joel Sartore/www.joelsartore.com, 46-47, 168-169; Charles Gurche, 50-51, 137; Joslyn Art Museum, Omaha, Nebraska, 53; Yale University Art Gallery, 56, 140, 184; Denver Public Library, Western History Department, 56-57; Courtesy South Dakota State Historical Society–State Archives, 63; Tom Bean 65, 88-89; The Granger Collection, New York, 70-71; Carr Clifton, 73, 110-111, 182-183; Courtesy Library of Congress, 77 (LC-USZ262 66856), 108 (LC-USZ62-114798); Courtesy Hillary & Megan Thompson, 78-9, 83, 90, 91; Sam Abell, NGP 84-85; Cumberland County Historical Society, Carlisle, PA 76 (photo by J. N. Choate), 96, 97, 101, 102-103; Art Resource, 104-105; Courtesy Little Bighorn Battlefield National Monument, National Park Service, 109, 127, 129 (upper); Image Bank/Getty Images), 116-117; University of Nebraska Press 120-121; Howard Terpning, Courtesy The Greenwich Workshop, Inc., 132-133; Paul Chesley/NG Image Collection, 138-139; Paul Chesley, 149, 192-193; Alan Slickpoo, 146; Bates Littlehales, 154-155; Edward S. Curtis/NG Image Collection, 156; Frederic Remington, Thomas Gilcrease Institute of American History & Art, 166-167; Courtesy Nevada Historical Society, 173; Eric Hasse/Contact Press Images, 176-177.

INDEX

Boldface indicates
illustrations.

A

A'aninin Gros Ventre Indians 7

Adobe Walls, Battle of (1874) 32, 81

American bison 4–5, 16–17, 42–47; uses 45, 53, 55, 195

Apache Indians 38–39, 135

Arapaho Indians: battles 44–45, 65–67; delegations 8–9, 19; Ghost Dance 174, 175; home area 50–51; peace talks 48–49, 71–72; as prisoners 82–83; treaties 26; unrest 43, 61, 81, 107

Arikara Indians 113, 114, 124, 126, 128, 128, 129, 129

Assiniboin Indians 32, 33; medicine signs 53

B

Bad Heart Bull, Amos: pictograph by 120–121

Badlands, S.Dak. 110–111, 184

Bannock Indians 147

Barnum, P. T. 32

Benteen, Frederick 118, 119, 122, 124

Big Dawn (Nez Perce warrior) 141

Big Foot (Miniconjou chief) 12, 178, 188–189, 190, 191, 194

Big Head, Kate 122–123

Big Hole Valley, Mont. 146–147, 149

Big Rascal (Cheyenne Indian) 66

Bighorn Mountains, Wyo. 72, 124

Bison see American bison

Black Coyote (Miniconjou Indian) 189

Black Elk (Oglala holy man) 115

Black Hills, S.Dak.-Wyo. 106, 106, 108–109

Black Horse (Cheyenne warrior) 82, 154, 158–159, 162–163, 167, 170

Black Horse (Comanche chief) 83

Black Kettle (Cheyenne chief) 40–41, 44–45, 48–49, 52, 65, 70–71, 72

Black Moon (Sioux chief) 179

Blackfeet Indians 55, 115, 118–119

Blodgett Canyon, Mont. 142–143

Bloody Knife (Arikara scout) 127

Bodmer, Karl: painting by 53

Bouyer, Mitch 114, 129

Bozeman, John 67

Bozeman Trail 9, 62–63, 67, 68–69, 70, 72, 74

Brady, Mathew: photograph by 108

Bridgeman, John 75

Brooks, Noah 31

Brown, Frederick 64–67

Buffalo see American bison

Buffalo Bill's Wild West Show 184, 185, 188

Buffalo Wallowing Woman (Cheyenne Indian) 163

C

Caddo Indians 8, 19, 82–83

Calhoun, James 157

Campbell, Ben Nighthorse 82

Canada: as refuge 97, 145, 147, 157, 179

Carlisle Indian Industrial School, Carlisle, Pa. 9, 76, 98, 100; students 102–103

Carrington, Henry B. 62, 63, 64–66

Catlin, George 32; paintings by 4–5, 33, 104–105

Cherokee Indians 8

Cheyenne Indians: Battle of Little Bighorn 115, 118–119, 123, 124, 150; battles 9, 43–45, 65, 67, 70–71, 72, 113; delegations 8–9, 19, 21, 52; home area 18, 50–51, 167, 170; map of paths northward 158; outbreak 158–159, 162–163, 166–167, 170; peace talks 48–49, 62–63, 71–72, 122; as prisoners 82–83, 86–87, 90–98; reservations 26,

157–158, 159, 166, 167, 170; unrest 43, 61, 81–82, 107, 109

Chivington, John M. 9, 45, 45, 48, 49, 52, 61

Civil War, U.S. 19, 21, 25–27, 32

Clark, W. P. 167, 170

Clark, William: purported son 140, 141

Cody, William F. 42, 184, 185

Colby, Leonard W. 191

Colby, Marguerite 191

Colley, Samuel G. 19, 21, 27, 31, 32, 43

Colorado Territory: unrest 25–26, 43–45, 61–62

Comanche Indians: delegations 8, 19; displacement 26; at Fort Sill, Okla. 56; peace talks 71–72; as prisoners 82–83, 86–87, 90–98; treaties 32; unrest 61, 70–71, 81

Coy (Kiowa Indian) 19, 30

Crazy Horse (Oglala Sioux chief) 9, 64, 65, 107, 113, 119, 120–121, 157

Crook, George 109, 113, 113

Crow Dog (Sioux chief) 185; camp 186–187

Crow Foot (Sitting Bull's son) 185, 188

Crow Indians 113–114, 124, 126, 130–131, 145, 150

Crow King (Sioux chief) 179

Curley (Crow scout) 114, 130–131

Curtis, Edward S. 49; photograph by 156

Curtis, Samuel R. 48

Custer, Boston 157

Custer, George Armstrong 108; Battle of Little Bighorn 97, 113, 118–119, 122–124, 157; Battle of the Washita 65, 70–71, 72, 119, 122; Black Hills Expedition 106, 108, 127; Cheyenne mistress 122–123; and Indian scouts 72, 114–115, 124, 126–131, 127; quarters 109

Custer, Libbie 108, 123

Custer, Tom 108, 157

D

Darlington Agency, Okla. 81–82, 157–158, 163, 170

Deas, Charles: painting by 10–11

Dole, William P. 27, 31, 45

Doolittle, James R. 67

Dull Knife (Northern Cheyenne Indian) 158, 163, 170, 171

E

Eastman, Charles 190

Eayre, George S. 43–44

Education 92–93, 95–98, 100

Elk horns 44, 151

Etla (Kiowa Indian) 19, 30

Evans, John 27, 43, 45, 48

F

Fetterman, William J. 64–67, 74

Fisher, Levando 166

Five Civilized Tribes 8

Fort Abraham Lincoln, N.Dak. 108, 126; officers and wives 109

Fort Hays, Kans. 122

Fort Laramie, Wyo. 58–59, 62–63

Fort Laramie Treaty of 1868 60, 67, 70, 74, 106, 108, 176

Fort Larned, Kans. 19, 71–72

Fort Larned Treaty of 1867 72

Fort Leavenworth, Kans. 48, 87; Indian agent 21

Fort Lyon, Colo. 27, 48–49

Fort Marion, St. Augustine, Fla. 9, 78–79, 80, 82, 86–87, 90–100; map of prisoners' route 86

Fort Phil Kearney, Wyo. 63–64, 72

Fort Robinson, Nebr. 163, 170; soldiers 166–167

Fort Sill, Okla. 56, 82, 83, 86–87, 98, 122

Fort Wise Treaty of 1861 26, 43, 44–45

G

Gall (Hunkpapa chief) 107, 118, 179

Gathering His Medicine (Cheyenne Indian) 163, 166

Geronimo (Apache chief) 179, 194

TRAIL TO WOUNDED KNEE

THE LAST STAND OF THE PLAINS INDIANS
1860-1890

HERMAN J. VIOLA

Published by the National Geographic Society

John M. Fahey, Jr.	President and Chief Executive Officer
Gilbert M. Grosvenor	Chairman of the Board
Nina D. Hoffman	Executive Vice President

Prepared by the Book Division

Kevin Mulroy	Vice President and Editor-in-Chief
Charles Kogod	Illustrations Director
Marianne R. Koszorus	Design Director

Staff for this Book

Barbara Brownell-Grogan	Executive Editor
Susan Tyler Hitchcock	Project and Text Editor
Cinda Rose	Art Director
Trudy Walker Pearson	Illustrations Editor
Carl Mehler	Director of Maps
XNR Productions	Map Research and Production
Eleanor Stables	Researcher
Janet Dustin	Illustrations Specialist
Gary Colbert	Production Director
Lewis Bassford	Production Project Manager
Elisabeth Booz, Margo Browning	Contributing Editors
Connie D. Binder	Indexer

Manufacturing and Quality Control

Christopher A. Liedel	Chief Financial Officer
Phillip L. Schlosser	Managing Director
John T. Dunn	Technical Director
Alan Kerr	Manager

Library of Congress Cataloging-in-Publication Data

Viola, Herman J.
    Trail to Wounded Knee : the last stand of the Plains Indians, 1860-1890 /
Herman J. Viola
            p. cm.
    Includes bibliographical references and index.
    1. Indians of North America–Great Plains–Wars. 2. Indians of North
America–Great Plains–Governmental relations. 3. Indians, Treatment
of–United States–History–19th century. 4. Red Cloud's War, 1866-1867.
5. Little Bighorn, Battle of the, Mont., 1876. 6. Wounded Knee Massacre,
S.D., 1890. 7. United States–Race relations. 8. United States–Politics and
government–19th century. I. Title.

    ISBN: 0-7922-2632-1 (regular)—ISBN 0-7922-2727-1 (deluxe)

One of the world's largest nonprofit scientific and educational organizations, the NATIONAL GEOGRAPHIC SOCIETY was founded in 1888 "for the increase and diffusion of geographic knowledge." Fulfilling this mission, the Society educates and inspires millions every day through its magazines, books, television programs, videos, maps and atlases, research grants, the National Geographic Bee, teacher workshops, and innovative classroom materials. The Society is supported through membership dues, charitable gifts, and income from the sale of its educational products. This support is vital to National Geographic's mission to increase global understanding and promote conservation of our planet through exploration, research, and education.

For more information, please call
1-800-NGS LINE (647-5463)
or write to the following address:

National Geographic Society
1145 17th Street N.W.
Washington, D.C. 20036-4688
U.S.A.

Visit the Society's Web site at
www.nationalgeographic.com.

Composition for this book by the National Geographic Book Division.
Printed and bound by R. R. Donnelly & Sons, Willard, Ohio.
Color separations by Quad Imaging, Alexandria, Virginia.
Dust jacket printed by the Miken Co., Cheektowaga, New York.

*Daylight Horse Capture holds her baby Red Willow near her home in Billings, Montana.
With her father, George Horse Capture, Senior Counselor to the Director at the Museum of
the American Indian, Daylight contributes to the Afterword, to tell the story of the American
Indian people from the massacre at Wounded Knee in 1890 to today.*

Afterword

✕

After the massacre at Wounded Knee, South Dakota, in 1890, where U.S. troops killed, according to tribal accounts, nearly 400 outnumbered Sioux Indian people, mostly women and children, and received 20 Congressional Medals of Honor for their deeds that cold day, many people believed the Indian world was over—finished. After all, the foreigners had been "removing" the natives of this hemisphere since Columbus set foot on our shining beaches. In many ways it was over—at least a special phase of our ancient traditional civilizations.

The People had suffered blow after blow from the newcomers, even from unseen things, like the germs of new diseases that exterminated millions. Not only had the tribes almost been wiped out, but the massive loss of their land base jeopardized the entirety of their existence. According to various estimates, between 7 and 15 million Indian people lived in what is now the United States in 1491. This figure drastically dropped to a critical 250,000 by 1910. A demographer says that if one adds the native birth rate over those five centuries to that initial estimate, the total loss of the Indian people far exceeds any other "extermination" in the Western world, even the Holocaust.

As the trails of broken treaties between the People and the Euro-Americans facilitated removal and land loss, the settlements of newcomers continued expanding westward, disturbing and destroying ancient cycles. Soon railroads had breached the continent, and the buffalo were suffering as badly as the Plains Indian people they nourished.

The People found themselves forcibly thrust into a new unfamiliar world not of their making. The world where they had lived and thrived for unknown centuries had vanished almost overnight. No longer could they freely move about following the buffalo. They now had to wait to be fed on the reservations by their captors, like animals. The newcomers violently changed everything; they even killed the horses in another effort to make the people dependent. With only a fragment of the people surviving, with all the great chiefs and even the medicine men removed, the tribes had no power. They could not even vote. They could do nothing but hunker down on the desolate reservations and survive. Their days of glory were over.

While adjusting to the dominating world of the white man, the People began to change. There was no other choice. They had to survive for the sake of their gallant ancestors and their future grandchildren. Different clothing began to be worn: cloth instead of supple deerskin. Wagons began replacing the travois. Then canvas wall tents, frame tents, and even log houses were seen instead of the beautiful tepees. New laws fashioned by white people far away changed the time-honored chief system, but the tribal leaders who emerged began to learn the new system and to lead their people into this new phase of our ongoing history. For the history of the people had to continue, and it did.

Developing forces continued to assault our tribal solidarity. Being part of a group—a tribe—one contributes strength, obligation, commitment, and allegiance to that group. In the old days, interactions with other groups were limited to trading or combat, so the tribe remained relatively intact. As their worlds contracted, the tribes were forced together against their will. These mixing bowls took many forms, some better than others. A seemingly benign mixing bowl created the most devastation among the people: the boarding school. Whether government or Christian—most were Catholic, these schools were not only painful, but lethal, inflicting long-term damage still felt today.

On many levels, government officials thought it would be good to send tribal children to boarding schools, whether or not the parents or children agreed. The schools were often in a tribally neutral area far from a student's home. Either the child had to stay in school year round or the parents had to travel vast distances to visit the young one, who probably wondered why the parents let this happen in the first place. Children who got too homesick often just started walking toward home. In winter, some froze to death on the way.

A standard boarding school greeting to new children involved cutting their long hair short and removing their tribal clothing for something more "civilized." Disorientation, shame, and pain quickly replaced pride and confidence. Elders still recall how the church people would hit and punish them for speaking their native language or crying. The children must have felt that their world was ending—and it was. The new world denied them the right to have a childhood and parents, so they could not learn how to be good parents, filled with love, intimacy, discipline, and all the rest. The students who made it home eventually married and had children, but they found to their horror that they did not know how to be good parents. In turn their children couldn't learn these essential skills. This loss plagues us to this day.

The traditional world of the American Indian people did end that frigid day in December 1890. It was a long time coming; the tribes had put up a gallant fight for their people and land against overwhelming numbers and technology. The massacre at Wounded Knee was the last major armed conflict between the tribes and the whites in North America, and a landmark in U.S. history. Historian Frederick Jackson Turner declared that the 1890 census failed to trace a moving frontier for the first time. The "winning of the West," as whites described the genocide of the Plains people, had been completed.

The phenomena we have endured since 1890 can be viewed in at least two different ways: as individual stories or as legislative history. Both views are important and instructive. Although the two views often overlap, I prefer the personal perspective.

The laws that have been enacted and the events that have occurred since 1890 have been too many and too important for a brief overview. For those who want a detailed inventory, I recommend "A History of Indian Policy," by S. Lyman Tyler, published by the U.S. Department of the Interior in 1973. The following are a few of those landmark pieces of legislation that dictated the way the People should live their lives.

1906	The Burke Act amends certain features of the Dawes Act that broke up unity of Indian land, and defines Indian "competency."
1907	The "Winter's Doctrine" defines the right of the U.S. to reserve water for the tribes.

Oklahoma is admitted to the Union as a state.
White citizens clamor to own Indian lands to increase the tax base.

1909   The Indian Health Program begins.

1917   A "new declaration of policy" liberalizing
        granting of titles for Indian land causes much Indian land loss.

1923   The Committee of One Hundred surveys and
        presents a report on "The Indian Problem."

1924   The U.S. Congress grants citizenship to the
        Indian people. Indian people did not get the right in all
        states to vote until 1948.

1928   The Merriam Report is published recommending
        massive reform of Indian Affairs.

1933   Actions are taken to emphasize the right of
        Indians to practice their own customs and religion.

1934   The Indian Reorganization Act reverses systems
        that break up tribal governments and land holdings typical
        of the allotment period.

1935   The Indian Arts and Crafts is established to assist tribal artists.

1944   The National Congress of American Indians, an advocacy
        group, is established by the tribes.

1946   The Indian Claims Commission is established to hear
        claims of tribes against the United States.

1948-53 The Relocation Program is established to move tribal workers
        to the cities and lower the population of reservations.

Scores of other pieces of legislation and actions have affected Indian lives, including the passage of the National Museum of the American Indian Act of 1989 that established the National Museum of the American Indian. These laws and actions fill volumes of publications. Each not only tells a story of the American Indian people but also defines our legal existence in this country. By studying these "procedures," one can detect the ambivalence that the non-Indian public feels toward the American Indian people. Perhaps some of that ambivalence may have its roots in how our legal status is defined in the United States. In "Cherokee Nation vs. Georgia" (1831) the Supreme Court under Chief Justice John Marshall ruled that tribes are not foreign but "domestic dependent nations." A year later in "Worcester vs. Georgia" the Court declared that only the federal government had the right to regulate affairs in Indian country. Andrew Jackson ignored the decision of the Supreme Court and had troops move the tribe from its land, resulting in the infamous

Trail of Tears to Oklahoma. Hundreds died en route. And so it went.

Later, after the tribes were nearly exterminated and their land almost lost, some people acknowledged that what happened to the American Indian people was wrong and felt remorse, guilt, or pity. Some laws became more just. However, even today, many groups still want whatever we managed to cling to—our remaining water, minerals, grass, fishing; even our sparse reservations.

All this can be viewed as a battle ground or a scoreboard as the many groups vie between themselves and the Indian people and their allies for these perceived assets. But we continue on the long road back

The word "epilogue" is not used here because one of its meanings is "end," and the world of the Indian people will never end. It will always exist in some meaningful form. This is vital not only to us but to other peoples. We represent an ideal in their minds, something no one else has but if everyone did the world would be a better place. It is a freedom, a connection to the universe, a perception of the unseen, a faith in what is around us, a belief in a people who do not march to the sound of money—a people who are friends with the Creator, and much more.

My years are many and the end of my road grows ever closer, but that is part of life's ancient cycle. In an effort to learn myself how a young Indian person views these things, I asked my daughter, Daylight, to tell me a part of her story, and she did:

"My earliest memories," wrote Daylight, "are of me and my older brother Joseph, first living in a big blue house, then fighting, then playing, then fighting again. It was fun. That's the way we showed affection. We grew up in Cody, Wyoming, a predominantly all-white town of 7,000 people, in northwest Wyoming, far from Indian people and our reservation.

In grade school I was always the odd person out and was teased because of my name or race. We were the only Indian family in town, and I had a few problems—sometimes I was called racist names—but Joseph took care of those rare incidences.

Being the odd person out at that age is never good. It undermines your confidence. I wanted always to fit in, as all adolescents do, and that was hard with a name like Daylight Horse Capture. Daylight belongs to my great-great-grandmother, Coming Daylight, and is such a pretty name. My Dad always tried to instill in my brother and me the pride of being Indian, and I felt something, but it wasn't exactly pride. Maybe it was uncertainty and shame.

I knew my family was different from others because we would go to powwows, which my Dad desperately wanted us to be a part of and enjoy. My brother and I both had our own dance regalia and tried to learn how to dance and act at powwows, but we always felt like we just didn't belong there. It is difficult to learn these things from the outside. Going to a powwow was fun in some ways. The people wearing all their fancy and beautiful outfits for the Grand Entry and the contests were the main attraction. But when it came down to us participating, there was always a dread because of the pressure we felt. I know that Dad meant well, but I guess he didn't understand that we were disconnected with the Indian world he knew, and we didn't feel part of it. My brother danced traditional and I danced traditional, then fancy, then jingle. I felt that I was absolutely no good at any of them.

Once my Dad put forth a "contest." This was an attempt to teach us some Indian ways, namely how to sing an Indian song. These are very difficult to learn because they have no titles or words. One must learn the "tune" and vocables. He said whoever could learn one Indian song in a year would be awarded a war bonnet, a great honor. My dad and I were always really close. Often I would sit on his lap in the living room and he would beat his hand drum and sing Indian songs to me. I was only five years old at the time and "daddy's little girl," but my mind was like a sponge. I amazed him when I became the first of his four children to know and sing an Indian song. This was not the plan, one of my older brothers was supposed to win that contest, but lo and behold, I did. There still is controversy as to where my war bonnet is.

I picked up quite a few Indian songs because my family went on a great deal of road trips. On these trips we would listen to tapes: Carly Simon, James Taylor, Paul Simon, and Willie Nelson were some of my dad's favorites, and I learned all those songs. But the Indian and 49 songs were the most fun. These songs have difficult sounds and words, and when you've finally learned them you've accomplished something.

My Dad worked at the museum in Cody and we would go there on weekends when it was empty. We would go into his office and he would get his drum and a tape player, and my younger brother Peter and I would listen to the tapes and the structure of the Indian songs, then attempt to sing them ourselves. We were pretty shy, while Dad wanted us to belt it out. When we did gather up enough courage to sing loudly at the right time, it would always bring a tear to his eye, and that was a good sign. Those are good memories.

In the summer of 1989 I got sick with lupus, which is an autoimmune disease, a horrible one that attacks the healthy tissue in the body, as if the immune system is deranged. I started on medicines and felt much better. But in little less than a year it returned. This time it was much worse. Lupus attacked my brain and my kidneys, rendering me unconscious for two days. The doctor increased my dosage, and even that wasn't controlling the flare. So the doctor started me on chemotherapy. Whoa. All of this happened around my 15th birthday. I gained a great deal of weight, lost much hair, and had a bad prognosis. They said I probably would never be able to have children and could well be sickly the rest of my life.

My dad, who had pledged and completed his four Sun Dances years earlier in his life, is a strong believer in the power of the sacred Plains Indian ceremony. Four days and nights without food or water while one prays and dances to the Creator is much more powerful than putting a dollar bill in the church basket on Sundays. The Creator listens more readily to your prayers. In an effort to secure spiritual assistance when the medicine failed, my dad explained the dire situation to my older brothers, Junior and Joseph, and they immediately pledged to do four Sun Dances if the Creator would help me. So every summer for four years the family, and friends who needed help, headed for the ceremonial grounds and set up camp. After the pledgers went into the lodge on the first evening, the women and others in the camp took care of the rest of the duties: cooking, cutting reeds, and performing all the necessities for the next four days. Everyone who attends this sacred ceremony benefits in some way, as the Creator pays close attention to the sacrifices and prayers. When it was over, our prayers were answered. I haven't been sick with lupus in 14 years. Now that is faith and power. This experience brought me much closer to our culture and sacred ways.

Soon after my second flare, my Dad was convinced that he was going to die soon because he had had two heart attacks, complicated by diabetes. Actually, he has been convinced of that off and on for about 14 years. He wanted to move closer to home, which is the Fort Belknap Indian Reservation, and he wanted my brother Joseph and me to be closer to our people. At last we settled in Hays, Montana, which is 35 miles south of the Agency, where my brother Junior lives.

Attending school on an Indian reservation was a very difficult thing to do. I had never been in a school before where the total enrollment was Indian students. I had never really gotten to know any Indian person close up before, only my family. Dealing with a new school and recovering from my lupus made for a difficult time. But it had to be done, and I did eventually make friends and my health continued to improve. These times on the reservation were very special and vital to my life, even though I didn't know it then. This is where the Horse Capture land has been located since the beginning.

For the first time in my life I was around people who had the same heritage and color as me and weren't amazed by my name. I still was an oddity because I liked school, but being an oddity for your chosen beliefs rather than because of your race and name, which you did not choose, is acceptable. I was lucky enough to be valedictorian when I graduated from the Hays/Lodge Pole High School. I now had my diploma and a lifelong bond with my people. I had accepted my Indian reality and was ready to move forward.

From high school I went straight to the University of Montana, which proved to be a mistake. I chose to party and bond with my Indian friends, which was much more fun than studying. All us Indians knew each other well and hung out—well, at least all the Rez Indians. I was a Reservation Indian now, a special class. Needless to say, I didn't make it past one semester.

I was never taught to be racist and I never was. Toward the end of my time in Missoula I befriended an African American basketball player and we grew close. We moved to Billings and later had a little boy together.

I was with my son's dad for three and some half years. During that time I fell out of touch with my people. I think this happened because I had heard negative stories about the relationship between Indian people and Blacks, and I wasn't going to allow anyone to treat my child unfairly.

After I left my son's dad I was really on my own, and I started going back to school. Being mostly alone in such a big city with no family was hard. I found myself still in the habit of checking out the Indians who were around. Through school I was able to make Indian friends, and some of them became my family. They would babysit, be roomies, and just be there. Although it was hard work, with the help of these friends, who were mostly single mothers as well, I was able to attend school and take care of my son.

When my son was three, I met a Cree man and we had a relationship for a while, resulting in my daughter. Several times when my children were young my skin would act up and I couldn't take proper care of them. My daughter was with her dad for much of her first year and, off and on, my son was with my older brother in Hays.

But after I got on my feet I retrieved my daughter, then my son, and now we all live together in Billings where we still endure some racial taunts, but live fairly normal lives.

Now that we are on our own, I find that I am the most comfortable when I am around my own people. This idea was totally foreign to me until I lived on the reservation and went to college with them. My choice is to be around my people. Eventually, after I get a college degree, I plan to attend law school and to help my people in some way—to help them find more of a voice. Having lived in both worlds will better enable me to do so.

When I was younger and lived in Cody, I didn't understand the importance of my heritage as I do now. My dad taught me the basic tools of understanding, and I consider myself very lucky to have been raised in this manner. I hope to carry those teachings to my own children. One can live in the city and still be a Rez Indian."

As I close this essay, I will share a recent experience with Daylight that I think gives insight into how today's Indian young people are set up as carriers of our traditions for future generations to hold and to share.

In mid-May 2004, Daylight and I were having one of our frequent phone conversations, and she mentioned a couple of Indian boys she knew who were working on a CD of 49-Indian songs. These are bright, quick, and contemporary Indian-style songs with alternating English and Indian vocables. Indian young people hold each other and dance to these songs, which have been around at least since WWII but are becoming more and more popular because they blend the Indian musical style with non-Indian words. One of Daylight's singing friends came to the city from the Fort Peck Indian Reservation in Montana; the other from Fort Washakie in Wyoming. She says these young native musicians are full of energy, expert at the electronic technology involved, and have beautiful voices.

Midway through her description her voice quickened, and I could hear her approaching excitement. She said the boys invited her and some other Indian people to sit in on one of their recording sessions that usually took place in someone's living room. One of them had a hand drum, and with a small drumstick he started the brisk, throbbing 49 beat. Their voices blended perfectly and clearly, carefully following their own composition.

Daylight describes the scene: "As the handsome Indian men began to drum and sing, their clear, vibrant voices filled the pulsating air. As we traveled along in their song, it lifted and carried us into a different place filled with Indianness, history, rhythm, tradition, and pure joy. I felt myself flying high above, floating, filled with happiness and pride. Filled with emotion I let go and wept, declaring to the world: Thank God for making me Indian."

So although the traditions are changing, they are also surviving. When our children feel this dedication, they appreciate themselves and what they are, and they will pass this gift to their children. They will keep the faith. And we will survive as Indian people, adding another phase to our ongoing history.

A view of the times happened recently when a reservation tribal executive joked, "Long ago when we came to Washington, D.C., to talk, we brought our war bonnet and buckskin clothing. Today when we make the same trip, we bring our briefcase and two tribal lawyers."

As for me, upon reflection, I would rather be in full warrior paint, astride my spotted pony, racing across the prairie, chasing the cavalry.

— GEORGE HORSE CAPTURE
— DAYLIGHT HORSE CAPTURE

TRAIL TO
Wounded Knee

AMERICAN TRAGEDIES

The Plains Indians stand forth, proud, strong, and resourceful, the very image of the American West. Yet in one of the most painful ironies of our history, their ancient culture was decimated in a single generation, through three decades of bitter warfare, chronicled in this powerful book.

Between the end of the Civil War and the final conquest of the frontier, U.S. Army soldiers and Indians collided again and again, in the Sand Creek Massacre, the Battle of the Washita, the Battle of the Little Bighorn, and in other fierce chases, retreats, and clashes, culminating in the devastating massacre of Big Foot's village at Wounded Knee in December 1890.

This eloquent volume—filled with vivid illustrations, historic photographs, and informative maps and written by a scholar and advocate of American Indians—depicts a brave world and its violent end.

ISBN 0-7922-8223-X

51600

9 780792 282235

$16.00 U.S./$23.00 Canada

ILLUSTRATIONS: (ABOVE) HERMAN VIOLA AND GEORGE HORSE CAPTURE
STUDY A DRAWING BY RED HORSE DEPICTING LITTLE BIGHORN: DANE
PENLAND, SMITHSONIAN INSTITUTION. (FRONT COVER) TEPEES: HERMAN
VIOLA; SKY: CORBIS; SITTING BULL: CORBIS; CUSTER: MEDFORD
HISTORICAL COLLECTION/CORBIS.